Word Strategies

Building a Strong Vocabulary
Low-Intermediate Level

Janet Giannotti
Northern Virginia Community College

New Readers Press

Word Strategies, Low-Intermediate Level
ISBN 978-1-56420-523-0

Copyright © 2007 New Readers Press
New Readers Press
Division of ProLiteracy Worldwide
1320 Jamesville Avenue, Syracuse, New York 13210
www.newreaderspress.com

Printed in the United States of America
9 8 7 6 5 4 3 2 1

All proceeds from the sale of New Readers Press materials
support literacy programs in the United States and worldwide.

Developmental Editor: Paula L. Schlusberg
Creative Director: Andrea Woodbury
Illustrations: Linda Tiff
Production Specialist: Jeffrey R. Smith

Contents

To the Student 5

To the Teacher 6

Lesson 1: Public Education 8

Lesson 2: Crime 18

Lesson 3: The Federal Government 28

Lesson 4: Entertainment 38

Lesson 5: Cars 48

Lesson 6: Health Care 58

Lesson 7: Banking 68

Lesson 8: Computers 78

Lesson 9: Transportation 88

Lesson 10: Advertising 98

Answer Key 108

To the Student

Sometimes you say, "I know that word."

What does this mean? When you know a word, you know a lot about the word, and you can do a lot with it.

- You can read the dictionary definition of the word and understand it.
- If the word has an abbreviation or shortened form, you know it.
- If the word is part of an initialization, you know the initialization. Initializations are short forms of two or more words, using the first letters of the words.
- You can add a prefix to the word to change the meaning.
- You can add a suffix to the word to change the part of speech.
- You understand the spelling changes that occur when you add a suffix to the word.
- You can think of one or more close synonyms for the word.
- You can think of an antonym, or opposite, for the word.
- You can use the word in a collocation. Collocations are fixed phrases of two or more words that are used together in a particular order.
- You understand fine points of meaning and grammar so that you do not confuse the word with similar words.
- You know how the word works in the context of other words.
- You know what part of speech the word is, even if you are not sure of the exact meaning.
- You can select the appropriate definition of the word from a list in your dictionary, even if the word has several definitions.

As you can see, there are many ways you can know a word. You can know a word to different degrees as well. You can simply guess the general meaning of the word. You can look up a word quickly in a dictionary. You can change a word with prefixes and suffixes. Or, you can quickly bring to mind a synonym or an antonym.

Word Strategies will help you know words better. The two-book set allows you to get to know hundreds of words in all of the ways outlined above. The first book presents words from your everyday life, including words about learning a language, shopping, job hunting, and TV. The second book presents more specialized words on subjects like the federal government, crime, computers, and health care. By completing both books, you can improve your vocabulary for school, work, and your everyday life.

To the Teacher

Welcome to *Word Strategies.* This two-book set has been designed to increase your students' word knowledge in all the ways outlined in "To the Student."

Each contextualized lesson begins with a short **reading** that presents the first dozen words of the lesson. In the first book (high-beginning level), the readings alternate between dialogs and simple narratives. In the second book (low-intermediate level), narratives alternate with expository readings. In the readings and throughout the exercises, students should be encouraged to use their learner's dictionaries to look up unfamiliar words that are not overtly taught in the lesson.

After the reading, students are asked to match the words with dictionary **definitions.** This should be an easy exercise that familiarizes students with the wording of dictionary definitions. The definitions presented here fit the way a word is used in the lesson's reading exactly. Later in the lesson, students work with their dictionaries to choose the best definition of a word in context.

The next part of the lesson presents students with **initializations** or **abbreviations** associated with the context. In some lessons, you may wish to extend this section with realia. For example, newspaper advertisements for cars, computers, or banks and financial services may contain initializations or abbreviations. Supermarket ads and weather reports can also be used. Or, students can search the Internet or use a map for weather, airport, and state abbreviations.

The first book then presents a section on **compound words.** Students who struggle with vocabulary may not realize that longer words are often made up of smaller, well-known words. Studying compounds can increase vocabulary and help students with their spelling.

Following that, both books have a section called **word building.** This section teaches students **prefixes** that change the meanings of words and **suffixes** that change the forms of words. This section also deals with spelling changes that occur when suffixes are added.

Each lesson then has an exercise on either **synonyms** or **antonyms.** Complete knowledge of a word allows students to access both synonyms and antonyms quickly. Some of the pairs in these exercises may seem easy; the purpose of this section is not specifically to build knowledge of pairs of words as much as it is to build facility in retrieving synonyms or antonyms.

After that, students focus on several **collocations,** or fixed phrases, associated with the context. For example, they learn that in American English, we attend a concert in a concert *hall,* but we attend a movie in a movie *theater.* The words in collocations always occur in a set order, so students learn to say we will have the picnic *rain or shine,* not *shine or rain.* They also work with collocations that involve common verbs like *pay* or *take,* in combination with prepositions.

The next section deals with **confusing words.** In this section, students should discuss fine distinctions between pairs of words. Some words in this section are content words that are similar in meaning, such as *teach* and *learn,* or *see* and *watch.*

Others are function words or phrases, like *a few* and *a little,* or *very* and *too.*

After that, students learn about context. Even the most comprehensive vocabulary program can't teach every word students will come across. Therefore, they need to practice relying on context. The first book asks students to rely on the most typical type of **context clue,** which is often identified as *general description.* While this section may feel like vocabulary review to students, these exercises train them to look at rich context as they read sentences and to choose words to complete those sentences. In the second book, students are introduced to other types of context clues, including noticing definitions or defining examples after dashes, and finding signals that indicate whether pairs of words are synonyms or antonyms.

The last two sections get students ready to use their dictionaries efficiently to look up words. When a student encounters an unfamiliar word, the first step is to identify the

part of speech—the way the word is working in that particular context. This can be a challenge in English, since many words serve double duty as nouns and verbs, as verbs and gerunds, as verbs and adjectives, and as adjectives and adverbs. Controlled exercises help students become more confident in recognizing parts of speech.

Finally, students are asked to look up words in a **dictionary.** Words in this exercise have been chosen because they have multiple meanings. It is the students' job to choose the best definition for the way the word is used in context. This is not a simple exercise and may best be done in class with large dictionaries that you provide, or with an online dictionary.

Each lesson ends with two review exercises: a **crossword puzzle** and a **vocabulary in context** exercise. These two activities recycle many of the words in the lesson.

An answer key appears at the end of each text.

Public Education

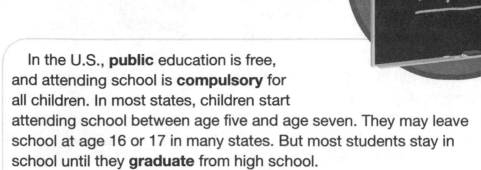

In this lesson, you will work with words about schools. Read this short description of public education in the U.S.

In the U.S., **public** education is free, and attending school is **compulsory** for all children. In most states, children start attending school between age five and age seven. They may leave school at age 16 or 17 in many states. But most students stay in school until they **graduate** from high school.

Each state makes its own rules about school, so the rules vary from state to state. For many children, school starts when they are five years old. That is when they attend **kindergarten.** Kindergarten primarily helps **prepare** children for learning. After that, most children spend five years in **elementary school**. In elementary school, children of the same age stay together in the same grade. They stay in one classroom with one teacher all day. Elementary school students start to study academic **subjects** like reading, math, and science.

At about grade 6, students move into middle school (or junior high school). The grades vary from one school system to another. It may be grades 6 through 8, or 7 through 9, or even 6 through 9. Middle school students generally all study the same subjects.

After middle school, students go to high school. High school students can make some choices about what they study. If they plan to **enroll** in **college**, they may take mostly **academic** classes. If they plan to get a job after graduation, they may take **vocational** classes.

At age 16 (or 17 in some states), students may choose to drop out of high school. Dropouts do not receive high school diplomas. If they discover later that they need high school **diplomas**, they don't have to re-enroll in school. Instead, they may take the GED tests. *GED* stands for General Educational Development. People who take the GED must show knowledge of basic high school subjects: reading, writing, math, science, and social studies.

Definitions

Write each word or phrase next to its definition.

academic	diploma	graduate	public
college	elementary school	kindergarten	subject
compulsory	enroll	prepare	vocational

_____ 1. a grade for young children that introduces them to school

_____ 2. this describes something that you must do or that is required

_____ 3. an official piece of paper stating that a student has earned a degree or finished a course of study

_____ 4. having to do with school or what you learn in school

_____ 5. relating to a job or trade

_____ 6. to successfully finish required studies at a school or college

_____ 7. to officially join (usually used with school or classes)

_____ 8. a school that you go to after high school

_____ 9. a school for the first six to eight years of a child's education

_____ 10. an area of knowledge that you study in school

_____ 11. provided for all of the people in a community

_____ 12. to get ready or make ready

Initializations

Match each initialization with what
it stands for.

Initializations are short forms of two or more words. We
use many initializations when we talk about school. You
can explain these initializations with sentences using
stands for.

_____ 1. GED   a. Associate in Arts (degree)

_____ 2. PE   b. digital versatile disk or digital video disk

_____ 3. BS   c. English as a second language

_____ 4. DVD   d. date of birth

_____ 5. ESL   e. physical education

_____ 6. CD   f. Bachelor of Science (degree)

_____ 7. DOB   g. General Educational Development

_____ 8. AA   h. compact disk

Exercise 3: Word Builder

Prefix

Choose a word from the box, add *re-*
to it, and write it on the line. If the word
begins with a vowel, put a hyphen (-) between *re-* and the word.

The prefix *re–* can mean *again.* If you add *re–* to the
beginning of a verb, it often means *to do (that action)
again.*

built	enroll	play	set	write
charge	fill	read	take	

1. If you drop out of school, you can _____.

2. You should _____ the chapter if you don't understand it.

3. You can _____ the test if you don't do well.

4. I need to _____ the battery in my video camera.

5. After the school burned, they _____ it.

6. You can _____ the tape if you don't understand.

7. No one liked my essay, so I think I'll _____ it.

8. You should _____ the counter to zero when you finish.

9. You can _____ your water bottle when it is empty.

Suffixes

Study each rule. Then write the noun form of the verb in parentheses on the line.

Rule 1: If a word ends in *–te,* drop the *–e* and add *–ion.*
Example: operate + ion = operation

1. (graduate)   The _____ was on June 20.

2. (cooperate)   I appreciate your _____.

3. (concentrate)   Memorizing dates requires _____.

4. (abbreviate)   You can write an _____ here.

Rule 2: Add *–ion* to words that end with *–t.*
Example: inspect + ion = inspection

5. (subtract)   Do we use addition or _____?

6. (suggest)   Do you like my _____?

7. (interrupt)   Please excuse the _____.

8. (invent)   This is a new _____.

9. (correct)   She made a _____ on my paper.

Rule 3: If a word ends with *–uce,* drop the *–e* and add *–tion.*
Example: introduce + tion = introduction

10. (reduce)   They made a _____ in the tuition.

11. (produce)   That man is in charge of the _____.

12. (introduce)   We listened to the _____.

Rule 4: If a word ends with *–de,* drop the *–de* and add *–sion.*
For example, collide + sion = collision

13. (invade)   I read about the _____ in history.

14. (explode)   We created an _____ in science.

15. (divide)   Fourth graders learn _____.

16. (decide)   Let's make a _____.

Antonyms

Choose an antonym from the box for each underlined word and write it on the line.

formal	**optional**	**public**
noisy	**present**	**together**

1. The playground is _____ but the halls are <u>quiet</u>.

2. Children who aren't in _____ schools may go to <u>private</u> ones.

3. Sometimes we study _____, but other times we are <u>apart</u>.

4. Until you are 16, school is not _____; it is <u>compulsory</u>.

5. Last week, the child was _____ two days and <u>absent</u> three.

6. Education includes both _____ and <u>informal</u> learning.

Collocations

English uses many collocations with prepositions to talk about school.

Choose a word from the box and write it on the line. Words can be used more than once.

by	**of**	**out**	**up**
from	**off**	**to**	

1. Students are free to discuss many topics that come _____ in high school.

2. Children are often dropped _____ by parents if they don't ride the bus.

3. The teacher checks _____ each name on her list when she takes attendance.

4. Many schools operate _____ September through June.

5. Rich and poor students often study side _____ side in public schools.

6. Public schools can vary _____ one state _____ another.

7. Too many students drop _____ _____ high school nowadays.

8. The teacher handed _____ books on the first day of class.

Confusing Words

Write a form of *spend* or *take* on each line. Use present or past tense.

Spend and *take* are both used to talk about using time. They work differently in sentences. For example, we say, "I spend (time)." But we say, "It (something) takes me (time)."

1. How much time did it _____ you to do your homework?

2. She _____ 45 minutes on the phone last night.

3. It _____ me more than two years to get my AA degree.

4. How long do the GED tests _____?

5. Did you know that it _____ several years to learn a language?

6. How much time do you _____ doing homework?

7. It _____ me an hour to get to school by bus.

8. I _____ my time on the bus wisely, doing homework.

Write a form of *spend* or *waste* on each line. You may use present or past tense.

Spend and *waste* are both used to talk about time and money. While *spend* just means *to use time or money*, *waste* means *to use more time or money than you need(ed) to.*

9. That movie wasn't good. I _____ my money on the ticket.

10. She gets good grades because she _____ at least one hour studying every night.

11. Frank brings his lunch to school. That way he only has to _____ about two dollars a day on coffee.

12. Tara studied the wrong chapter last night. She _____ an hour doing that. Now she has to study the correct chapter.

13. Don't _____ your time at that movie. It isn't worth it.

14. How much time do you usually _____ studying? It takes me about an hour to study for a test.

ext Clues

...cle the vocabulary item (the word or
phrase that appears right before the dash). Then underline or highlight the
definition or defining examples. Write *definition* or *examples* on the line.

> In each of the following, words are defined in the context of the sentence. A definition or defining examples appear after a dash.

_____ 1. If you need information about the school, call the principal—the head of the school.

_____ 2. If you can't afford a university, you should consider a community college—a two-year public institution.

_____ 3. High school students study several subjects—math, science, history, English—every day.

_____ 4. High school students can take electives—music, art, drama—in addition to their academic subjects.

_____ 5. A child brings home a report card—a summary of grades and progress—four times a year.

_____ 6. Young students learn basic arithmetic—addition and subtraction.

_____ 7. You'll need a high school diploma if you want to move on to an institution of higher education—a college or university.

_____ 8. A student who is having trouble may need a tutor—a teacher who can work one-on-one with him or her.

_____ 9. If you don't graduate—recieve a diploma—you may have a hard time getting a job.

_____ 10. Informal learning takes place in preschool—schooling before kindergarten, also called nursery school.

_____ 11. Some secondary schools are vocational schools—schools where students learn job skills.

_____ 12. A high school orchestra is usually made up of stringed instruments—violins, violas, cellos—and some percussion instruments.

_____ 13. Nowadays, most playground equipment—slides, swings, and climbers—needs to be accessible to children in wheelchairs.

_____ 14. Most elementary school children say that recess—the time they are allowed to go outside and play—is their favorite part of school.

Parts of Speech

Identify the underlined words. Write *N*
on the line if the word is a noun, and
write *V* if it is a verb.

Many common vocabulary words can work either as
nouns or as verbs. Look for a noun after an article or a
possessive. Look for a verb after a subject.

_____ 1. The teacher <u>promises</u> to give less homework.

_____ 2. The <u>work</u> gets harder in secondary school.

_____ 3. His report card tells about his <u>progress</u>.

_____ 4. Elementary schools <u>start</u> the day with "The Pledge of Allegiance."

_____ 5. Most children <u>progress</u> through the grades without repeating.

_____ 6. I kept my <u>promise</u> about doing my homework on time.

_____ 7. When a student completes her <u>studies</u>, she receives a diploma.

_____ 8. Most schools have announcements at the <u>start</u> of every day.

_____ 9. Some students <u>work</u> on community service projects.

_____ 10. A typical high school student <u>studies</u> three hours every night.

Dictionary

Identify the part of speech of each underlined word or phrase. Write *N*
or *V* on the line. Then look up the word in your dictionary. Choose and
write the best definition.

_____ 1. My favorite subject is <u>social studies</u>.

definition: _____

_____ 2. Kindergarteners have a <u>snack</u> every morning.

definition: _____

_____ 3. I'm looking forward to my high school <u>reunion</u>.

definition: _____

_____ 4. You should apply for a <u>scholarship</u>.

definition: _____

_____ 5. The dates of spring break <u>vary</u> from year to year.

definition: _____

Crossword Puzzle

Fill in the puzzle with words from the box.

absent	diploma	GED	principal	subject	vary
attend	drop	off	reunion	takes	vocational
college	ESL	playground	snack	tutor	

ACROSS

3. If you need extra help, hire a private _____.
5. Many high school graduates plan to attend _____.
7. The _____ is the head of the school.
11. You receive your _____ when you graduate.
12. I attend a high school _____ every five years.
13. _____ stands for *General Educational Development.*
14. Algebra is a high school _____.
15. _____ stands for *English as a second language.*
16. She took attendance and checked _____ my name.
17. The children eat a _____ in the morning.

DOWN

1. Five-year-olds usually _____ kindergarten.
2. Students who don't finish school _____ out.
4. _____ classes teach job skills.
6. Laws about schools _____ from state to state.
8. If you are not in school you are marked _____.
9. They like to play on the _____ during recess.
10. It usually _____ four years to get a degree.

Vocabulary in Context

Choose a word from the box and write it on the line.

college	elementary	kindergarten	secondary	university

Most children enter _____ when they are five years old. After that, they spend

five years in _____ school. Then they move into _____
              1   2   3

school. If they want to continue their education after they finish high school, they can attend a

_____ or _____.
         4   5

re-enroll	replay	reread	retake	rewrite

It seems that Marla has to do everything twice these days. Yesterday, she didn't understand a

chapter in her book, so she had to _____ it. Then she was listening to a tape
                                         6

of the lecture and she couldn't hear it. She had to _____ the tape several
                                       7

times. Finally she had to _____ a composition that she wasn't happy with.
                             8

Next week, she is going to _____ a test that she failed. If things don't start
                             9

going better for Maria, she is going to have to _____ in the same class
                                    10

next year.

diploma	electives	graduation	schedules	subjects

Some high school students can set their own _____. They have to be careful
                                      11

to take all of the _____ that are required for _____. Some
            12   13

students would like to fill their days with _____ like art, drama, or driver's ed.
                                      14

If they want a _____, they have to take more academic classes.
            15

Crime

In this lesson, you will work with words about crimes. Read this story about a dangerous neighborhood.

Last year, Jessica moved into a new apartment. At first, Jessica liked her new home. That was before she discovered that she lives in a high **crime** neighborhood. The **criminals** don't live in Jessica's neighborhood. They just like to work there.

The first problem that Jessica noticed was **shoplifting**. There is a lot of shoplifting at the grocery store on her street. The owner uses cameras to try to catch the shoplifters. People put items into purses and backpacks. They put items under their clothes. Last week the police **arrested** two people. They were stealing steaks from the store. They each had four steaks under their shirts.

Vandalism is also a problem in Jessica's neighborhood. Sometimes people use spray paint to write on the walls of buildings. Once someone broke a lot of car windows. Another time someone broke the gate in front of Jessica's apartment building. It costs a lot to repair the damage done by the vandals.

Last month there was a **robbery** in the neighborhood. Someone entered a jewelry store with a gun and robbed the owner. The robber stole some money and some rings. The police are **investigating** that crime now. The **victim** wasn't hurt, but he is too scared to open his store now.

Jessica also heard that there was a **kidnapping** in the neighborhood last year. Two men in a black car kidnapped a young woman. The kidnapping happened right in the middle of a busy street. Several people **witnessed** the crime and called the police. Jessica heard that the police found the woman and her kidnappers. She hopes that they were **punished** for their crime.

Jessica is afraid that the next crime she hears about is going to be a **murder** or other violent crime. That is why she is looking for a new apartment now.

Definitions

Write each word next to its definition.

arrest	investigate	punish	vandalism
crime	kidnap	robbery	victim
criminal	murder	shoplift	witness

_____ 1. someone who sees a crime or accident and can describe what happened

_____ 2. to try to find out all of the information and facts about a crime or a problem

_____ 3. when the police take a person away because they think he or she broke a law

_____ 4. something that people do that is against the law

_____ 5. the person who is hurt in a crime

_____ 6. to take someone away illegally and by force and to hold him or her to get money or something else of value

_____ 7. the crime of killing a person

_____ 8. to cause someone to suffer because he or she did something wrong or broke the law

_____ 9. someone who is involved in illegal activities or who commits a crime

_____ 10. to take something from a store without paying for it

_____ 11. the crime of destroying or damaging property

_____ 12. the crime of stealing something from a person or a place, often with the use of force

Initializations

Match each initialization with what it stands for.

Initializations are short forms of long words or of two or more words. We often use initializations to talk about crime. You can explain these initializations with sentences using *stands for.*

_____ 1. aka

_____ 2. ASAP

_____ 3. DNA

_____ 4. DOA

_____ 5. HQ

_____ 6. ID

_____ 7. NA

_____ 8. PI

a. Dead On Arrival

b. Headquarters

c. As Soon As Possible

d. Identification

e. also known as

f. Not Available or Not Applicable

g. Private Investigator

h. Deoxyribonucleic Acid

Exercise 3: **Word Builder**

Prefix

Choose a word from the box, add *dis-* to it, and write it on the line.

The prefix *dis–* can mean *not.* If you add *dis–* to the beginning of a word, it makes the meaning negative.

advantage	connect	qualify
agree	honest	respectful

1. When Jessica moves, she will _____ her phone.

2. She and her neighbor _____ about the neighborhood. He thinks it's a great place to live and she hates it.

3. Crime is a big _____ to that neighborhood.

4. Some people aren't polite. They are _____.

5. _____ people often don't tell the truth.

6. They might _____ you from the race if you break the rules.

Suffix

Study each rule. Then fill in the gerund form of the verb in parentheses.

> The suffix *–ing* changes a verb into a gerund. A gerund works like a noun. We often use a gerund as the subject of a sentence.

Rule 1: If a word ends with a consonant-vowel-consonant (CVC) pattern, double the final consonant before adding *–ing*.
Example: stop + ing = stopping

1. (stop) _____ crime is the job of the police.

2. (rob) _____ banks is dangerous.

3. (hit) _____ people is against the law.

4. (run) _____ from the police is a bad idea.

Rule 2: If a word ends with a silent *–e*, drop the *–e* before adding *–ing*.
Example: investigate + ing = investigating

5. (investigate) _____ crimes is the detective's job.

6. (fine) _____ people is a way of punishing them.

7. (move) _____ to a new neighborhood is Jessica's only option.

8. (chase) _____ criminals is a police officer's job.

9. (fire) _____ a gun on a crowded street is dangerous.

Rule 3: For most other words, just add *–ing*.
Example: steal + ing = stealing

10. (steal) _____ is always illegal.

11. (shoplift) _____ is a crime.

12. (shoot) _____ a gun without a license is not legal.

13. (witness) _____ a crime can be scary.

14. (repair) _____ vandalized property is expensive.

15. (find) _____ a safe neighborhood is important.

16. (stay) _____ somewhere safe is essential.

Antonyms

Choose an antonym from the box for each underlined word and write it on the line.

death	lie	safe
freed	low	violent

1. The judge sentenced him to _____, not to <u>life</u> in prison.

2. He told a _____. He never told the <u>truth</u>.

3. They <u>arrested</u> him, but then _____ him the next day.

4. It was a _____ scene, not a <u>peaceful</u> one.

5. She wanted a _____ neighborhood but found a <u>dangerous</u> one.

6. She lives in a <u>high</u> crime area and is looking for a _____ crime neighborhood.

Collocations

English speakers use many two- and three-word collocations, some with *and*, when talking about crimes.

Choose a word from the box to complete each collocation below.

against	break	crime	jury
assault	cheat	house	punishment

1. He was guilty of _____ and battery.

2. Why do they have to lie, _____, and steal?

3. It's all about crime and _____.

4. In your home, you can be the judge and _____.

5. That's _____ the law.

6. Is bank robbery a victimless _____?

7. If you _____ the law, you go to jail.

8. The judge placed him under _____ arrest.

Confusing Words

In each of the following, circle the word that best completes the sentence.

Rob and *steal* are both crimes having to do with taking something that is not yours. *Rob* tells about the person or place from which something is taken, and *steal* tells about the thing that was taken. You *rob* a person or a place, but you *steal* a thing.

1. Ted (robbed/stole) a drug store.

2. Ms. Reed was (robbed/stolen) on the street.

3. They (robbed/stole) my new car.

4. Did someone (rob/steal) that painting?

5. Someone (robbed/stole) that gas station.

6. I thought that man was going to (rob/steal) me.

7. The famous thief (robbed/stole) that museum.

8. Some money was (robbed/stolen) from her purse.

Write a form of *drop* or *fall* on each line. Use present or past tense.

Drop and *fall* both tell about moving to a lower position. *Drop* means *to cause something to move to a lower position*, and *fall* describes the action in which something moves to a lower position.

9. The police officer yelled to the thief, "_____ the gun!"

10. Some of the stolen items _____ on the street as the shoplifter ran.

11. As he was running away, the shoplifter _____ on the sidewalk.

12. The robber _____ some of the money that he had just stolen.

13. The gun _____ out of his pocket.

14. The shoplifter _____ the steak when he ran.

15. The money _____ on the sidewalk as the bank robbers escaped.

16. The police officer tripped and _____ while chasing the thief.

Context Clues

Copy the two words or phrases with similar meanings in each of the following.

> When you guess from context, you can often find a word with a similar meaning in the same sentence. Look for words like *similar, same, and, both,* and the verb *to be* to show that a sentence contains words with similar meanings.

1. Burglars and robbers both steal things.

   _____   _____

2. Battery is similar to assault, so you can go to jail if you commit either one.

   _____   _____

3. Some people think shoplifting is a victimless crime, but it is the same as stealing.

   _____   _____

4. If you get arrested, you need a lawyer because you should never talk to the police without an attorney present.

   _____   _____

5. Killing someone can be considered murder.

   _____   _____

6. A gun is one weapon that most robbers own.

   _____   _____

7. If you shoot at a police officer, he or she may fire back at you.

   _____   _____

8. When you finish talking to that detective, another investigator wants to talk to you.

   _____   _____

9. The boys were charged with vandalism and destroying property.

   _____   _____

10. Stealing is against the law, and vandalism is illegal, too.

   _____   _____

Parts of Speech

Identify the underlined words. Write *N* on the line if the word is a noun, and write *V* if it is a verb.

Many common vocabulary words can work either as nouns or as verbs. Look for a noun after *the* or a preposition. Look for a verb after *to* or after a modal like *can*.

_____ 1. That novel is about <u>murder</u> and other crimes.

_____ 2. I can't <u>witness</u> a crime and stay silent.

_____ 3. The police are about to <u>arrest</u> that man.

_____ 4. They investigated the <u>murder</u>.

_____ 5. I don't want to <u>witness</u> a crime.

_____ 6. The criminal will <u>murder</u> someone.

_____ 7. There is a special room in the police station for <u>witnesses</u>.

_____ 8. The police should <u>arrest</u> her.

_____ 9. The police are going to make the <u>arrest</u> now.

_____ 10. They questioned the <u>witness</u>.

Dictionary

Identify the part of speech of each underlined word. Write *N* or *V* on the line. Then look up the word in your dictionary. Choose and write the best definition.

_____ 1. The police arrested that person for <u>battery</u>.

definition: _____

_____ 2. The criminal had to appear in <u>court</u>.

definition: _____

_____ 3. The officer was going to <u>shoot</u> the suspect.

definition: _____

_____ 4. The <u>fine</u> for vandalism could be $5,000.

definition: _____

_____ 5. The judge will decide the <u>sentence</u> after the trial.

definition: _____

Crossword Puzzle

Fill in the puzzle with words from the box.

AKA	criminal	fine	investigating	murder	victim
arrest	dishonest	fired	jury	sentenced	violations
burglar	DOA	HQ	kidnap	vandalism	witness

ACROSS

2. A _____ entered the house and stole something.
4. The judge _____ the criminal to life in prison.
9. People almost never go to jail for traffic _____.
10. The person who is hurt in a crime is the _____.
12. _____ stands for *headquarters.*
13. If you take him by force, you _____ him.
14. Money that you pay as a punishment is a _____.
15. The judge or the _____ can decide.
17. The police are _____ the crime.

DOWN

1. Destroying property is _____.
3. The police take you away when they _____ you.
5. A person who commits a crime is a _____.
6. A person who sees a crime is a _____.
7. _____ stands for *dead on arrival.*
8. A _____ person doesn't tell the truth.
11. Killing someone intentionally is _____.
16. A police officer _____ the gun.
18. _____ stands for *also known as.*

Vocabulary in Context
Choose a word from the box and write it on the line.

crime	murder	robbery	shoplifting	vandalism

Jessica lives in a high-_____ neighborhood. Since she has lived there, she
1

has noticed _____ in the local grocery store, and _____ to
2   3

some cars on the street. Once there was an armed _____ at the jewelry store.
4

Jessica just hopes she doesn't witness a violent crime like assault or _____.
5

disadvantages	disagrees	disconnected	dishonest	disrespectful

Jessica's apartment building has a lot of _____. First, her landlord is
6

_____. He tells her one thing but he does another. Once he even
7

_____ her cable TV service even though she paid her rent on time. Also,
8

some teenagers in the building are _____. They always make rude comments
9

to Jessica. Jessica's neighbor _____ with her. He thinks it's a great place to
10

live. But Jessica is sure she wants to move.

fired	gun	rob	shot	steal

One day, someone _____ a _____ in Jessica's neighborhood.
11   12

Jessica discovered that the jewelry store owner had been _____. Someone
13

was trying to _____ the jewelry store, but the robber didn't
14

_____ anything.
15

The Federal Government

In this lesson, you will work with words about the U.S. federal government. Read this description of the three branches of government.

In the U.S., the **federal** government is divided into three **branches**. The branches are interrelated. They **balance** each other.

One branch of the government is the legislative branch. The legislative branch is also called Congress. Each state sends elected officials to Washington, D.C. The officials **serve** in Congress. Congress is divided into two houses. Senators serve in the Senate. Representatives serve in the House of Representatives. Senators serve for six years, and representatives serve for two years. Both types of legislators can be re-elected. Senators and representatives often serve many **terms**. The legislative branch **proposes** and votes on new laws.

Another branch of the government is the executive branch. The executive branch **enforces** the laws. The president is the head of the executive branch. The president has the power to **veto** some decisions made by the legislative branch. The country **elects** a president every four years. A president can be re-elected one time.

The third branch of government is the judicial branch, or the courts. The highest court is the Supreme Court. There are nine judges on the Supreme Court. They are called justices. Supreme Court justices are **appointed** by the president. They are also **approved** by Congress. They serve for life—until they decide to retire or until they die. The justices explain and interpret the meaning of laws for the people.

The U.S. Constitution **created** the three branches of government. The people who wrote the Constitution wanted the branches to balance each other. The legislative branch proposes and votes on laws. The executive branch can veto those laws and send them back to the legislative branch. And the judicial branch can explain laws and decide whether those laws agree with the ideas in the Constitution.

Definitions

Write each word next to its definition.

appoint	branch	enforce	serve
approve	create	federal	term
balance	elect	propose	veto

_____ 1. to spend a period of time doing a job, usually in the government

_____ 2. to select someone by voting

_____ 3. to make people obey a law or rule

_____ 4. having to do with a central government of a country that contains more than one state

_____ 5. to formally suggest a plan

_____ 6. to officially refuse to allow something to happen, especially after another group has agreed

_____ 7. to officially accept a proposal

_____ 8. a part or division of government or another organization

_____ 9. to designate or choose someone to do a job or duty

_____ 10. a period of time that a person does a government job

_____ 11. to make equal so that one part is not more important or more powerful than another

_____ 12. to make something that did not exist before

Abbreviations

Match each abbreviation with the word
that it represents.

Many job titles and other words associated with the
government are abbreviated. When you read an
abbreviation, you say the whole word. For example,
when you read *Sen.*, before a person's name, you say
Senator.

_____ 1. Gov.   a. Vice President

_____ 2. Del.   b. Senator

_____ 3. D   c. Governor

_____ 4. Rep.   d. Democrat

_____ 5. dept.   e. government

_____ 6. govt.   f. department

_____ 7. Sen.   g. Republican

_____ 8. R   h. Delegate

_____ 9. VP   i. Representative

Exercise 3: Word Builder

Prefix

Choose a word from the box, add
inter– to it, and write it on the line.

The prefix *inter–* can mean *between or among two or
more things or people.*

city	continental	national	related
connected	dependent	office	state

1. The three branches are connected in many ways, so we say they are _____.

2. That _____ company does business in several countries.

3. The bus that goes from Chicago to New York is an _____ bus.

4. The trade between Europe and South America is _____ trade.

5. The three branches are related to each other, so we say they are _____.

6. Some plants and animals depend on each other, so we say they are _____.

7. A road that goes between states is called an _____ highway.

8. _____ mail goes between two or more offices in one organization.

Suffix

> The suffix *–ly* changes an adjective into an adverb. An adverb tells how an action is done.

Study each rule. Then fill in the adverb form of the adjective in parentheses.

> **Rule 1: If an adjective ends in *–al*, add *–ly*. This results in a double *l*.**
> **Example: national + ly = nationally**

1. (federal)   Some judges are appointed _____.

2. (national)   The president is elected _____.

3. (local)   Many decisions are made _____.

4. (personal)   The president doesn't enforce laws _____.

> **Rule 2: If an adjective ends in *–le*, drop the *–e* and add *–y*.**
> **Example: responsible + ly = responsibly**

5. (possible)   The president may _____ veto the proposal.

6. (remarkable)   _____, the unpopular senator was re-elected.

7. (responsible)   Judges must act _____.

> **Rule 3: If an adjective ends in a consonant and *–y*, change the *–y* to *–i* before adding *–ly*.**
> **Example: easy + ly = easily**

8. (happy)   The official _____ accepted the appointment.

9. (easy)   The president was re-elected _____.

10. (busy)   The senators are _____ working on new laws.

> **Rule 4: If an adjective ends in *–ic*, add *–ally*.**
> **Example: historic + ly = historically**

11. (patriotic)   He speaks _____ about his country.

12. (logic)   The justices work _____ through the problem.

13. (realistic)   Can a justice _____ serve his or her whole life?

14. (historic)   _____, all justices were men. Recently, however, some women have become justices.

Synonyms

Look at each underlined word. Choose a word from the box with a similar meaning and write it on the line.

agency	justice	recommendation
appointed	national	reject

1. The <u>Bureau</u> of ATF is the _____ that regulates alcohol, tobacco, and firearms.

2. The last president _____ two justices, and the current one <u>selected</u> two also.

3. Congress will discuss the president's _____ after the formal <u>nomination</u> is presented.

4. He was a <u>judge</u> in a lower court, and then he became a _____ on the Supreme Court.

5. The president <u>vetoed</u> the proposal and promised to _____ the next one as well.

6. Many agencies of the <u>federal</u> government are located in the _____ capital region around Washington, D.C.

Collocations

In each of the following, circle the word that best completes the sentence.

Hold and *take* are general verbs that are used in many collocations.

1. The committee is (holding/taking) a meeting today.

2. New laws often (hold/take) effect on January 1.

3. The new president (holds/takes) office on January 20.

4. He hopes to be elected, but no one knows what the future (holds/takes).

5. That country will (hold/take) elections next year.

6. The candidate (held/took) credit for a lot of the improvements.

Confusing Words

In each of the following, write *capital* or *capitol* on the line.

> *Capital* and *capitol* are both used to talk about the government, but they have different meanings. A *capital* is a city where the government of a state or country is located. A *capitol* is the building where the people who make the laws meet.

1. He took an elevator to his office on the fourth floor of the _____.

2. Is Chicago the _____ of Illinois?

3. When we drove through the city at night, we noticed that there were some lights on in the _____.

4. If you live in the _____ of the U.S., you might see the president.

5. The representative parks in a garage near the _____ and walks up to his office.

6. Often the _____ of a state is not the largest city in that state.

7. We took a bus tour of the _____. We drove past all of the important buildings.

In each of the following, write *principle(s)* or *principal(s)* on the line.

> *Principle* and *principal* sound the same but have different meanings and can be different parts of speech. *Principle* is a noun that means *a basic idea or belief*. *Principal* can be an adjective that means *main* or *most important*. It can also be a noun that means *the person in charge of a school*.

8. The teacher talked to the _____ about the student.

9. The _____ job of the legislative branch is to make laws.

10. The Constitution outlines the basic _____ that guide the government.

11. Income taxes are the country's _____ source of income.

12. I don't understand the general _____ on which the idea is based.

Context Clues

Copy the two words or phrases with opposite meanings in each of the following.

When you guess from context, you can often find a word with an opposite meaning in the same sentence to help you. Look for words like *different, but,* or *while* to show that a sentence contains words with opposite meanings.

1. Senators are elected, while judges are appointed.

   _____   _____

2. Two proposals were rejected, but one was accepted.

   _____   _____

3. Working for local government is different from working for the federal government.

   _____   _____

4. Some people think businesses are too regulated, but others think businesses are free to do what they want.

   _____   _____

5. The president fired one advisor, but the other one resigned.

   _____   _____

6. Some committee meetings are boring, but others are interesting.

   _____   _____

7. The president agrees with some ideas, but is opposed to others.

   _____   _____

8. He was pleased with the process, but disappointed in the outcome.

   _____   _____

9. During the crisis, the president was calm while his advisors seemed troubled.

   _____   _____

10. One candidate seems to be aware of the problems, while his opponent seems to be ignorant of the issues.

   _____   _____

Parts of Speech

Identify the underlined words. Write *V*
on the line if the word is a verb, and
write *Adj.* if it is an adjective.

> Many common vocabulary words that end in *–ed* can
> work either as verbs or as adjectives. Look for a verb
> after a subject and before an object. Look for an
> adjective before a noun.

_____ 1. The last president <u>appointed</u> several judges.

_____ 2. The president is an <u>elected</u> official.

_____ 3. Supreme Court justice is an <u>appointed</u> position.

_____ 4. That agency <u>regulated</u> banking during the 1930s.

_____ 5. The committee <u>proposed</u> several laws.

_____ 6. A bill is a <u>proposed</u> law.

_____ 7. The president <u>nominated</u> several officials.

_____ 8. The class <u>elected</u> a representative for the student council.

_____ 9. Interstate shipping is a <u>regulated</u> industry.

_____ 10. The president <u>vetoed</u> that proposal.

Dictionary

Identify the part of speech of each underlined word. Write *N, V,* or *Adj.* on the line.
Then look up the word in your dictionary. Choose and write the best definition.

_____ 1. My neighbor was just elected to the county <u>board</u> of supervisors.

definition: _____

_____ 2. The secretary of state is a member of the president's <u>cabinet</u>.

definition: _____

_____ 3. The First Amendment <u>guarantees</u> freedom of speech.

definition: _____

_____ 4. A <u>naturalized</u> citizen cannot be elected president.

definition: _____

_____ 5. Which government <u>agency</u> does he work for?

definition: _____

Crossword Puzzle

Fill in the puzzle with words from the box.

agency	capitol	enforce	justice	serve
appoints	effect	federal	principle	takes
balances	elect	govt.	Rep.	term
branches	elections	holds	Sen.	vetoes

ACROSS

2. This country holds _____ every November.
4. If the president rejects it, he _____ it.
6. The president _____ his advisors.
11. The abbreviation for *Representative* is _____.
12. The executive branch must _____ the laws.
15. There are three _____ of government.
16. We _____ the president every four years.
17. The senators work in the _____ building.
19. A Supreme Court judge is called a _____.
20. A government office is often called an _____.

DOWN

1. _____ is the abbreviation for *government*.
3. A senator serves a _____ of six years.
5. _____ is the abbreviation for *Senator.*
7. A _____ is a belief on which a system is based.
8. The _____ government is in Washington, D.C.
9. No one knows what the future _____.
10. A president can only _____ two terms.
13. New laws often take _____ on January 1.
14. Each branch of the government _____ another.
18. The new president _____ office in January.

Vocabulary in Context

Choose a word from the box and write it on the line.

appointed	elected	nomination
approve	justices	selects

Supreme Court _____ aren't _____; they are
               1   2

_____ by the president. First, the president _____ a judge to
   3   4

become a justice. Then Congress must _____ the _____.
                                  5   6

After that, the judge becomes a Supreme Court justice.

effect	elections	office	officials

In the U.S., _____ are held every November. Sometimes people vote on new
            7

laws. The laws generally take _____ the year after the election. In most
                             8

elections, government _____ are chosen. They generally take
                          9

_____ in January of the following year.
   10

Intercity	interstate	interconnected	international

_____ travel became easier in the 1950s when the federal government
     11

created the _____ highway system. Now all of the cities in the country are
             12

_____ by a big network of highways. Some of those highways are even
   13

_____, since they lead to either Canada or Mexico.
   14

Entertainment

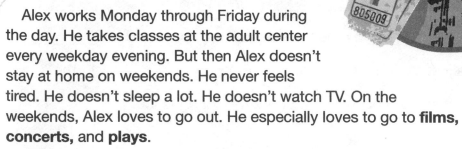

In this lesson, you will work with words about entertainment. Read this story about the forms of entertainment that Alex enjoys.

Alex works Monday through Friday during the day. He takes classes at the adult center every weekday evening. But then Alex doesn't stay at home on weekends. He never feels tired. He doesn't sleep a lot. He doesn't watch TV. On the weekends, Alex loves to go out. He especially loves to go to **films, concerts,** and **plays**.

Last month, Alex saw several films. There was an international film festival at a theater **downtown**. Alex **purchased** tickets for the series of six films. He enjoyed all of them, but he thought the Italian film and the Indian film were the best. Every day that he attended the festival, Alex took a bus downtown. He stopped in a restaurant for dinner after each film. Alex invited several friends to see the films with him. Everyone enjoyed the festival.

Alex likes going to films, but he likes live **performances** better. Last month, Alex attended two concerts. The first one was at the concert **hall** on the college campus. Alex heard a symphony **orchestra**. They played some pieces by Mozart and Beethoven. The second concert was in a **club** near Alex's apartment. He heard a jazz **band** play at the club. Alex thought the saxophones and the trumpets were the best instruments in the band. Some people were dancing in the club, but Alex prefers just to listen to the music.

In addition to concerts, another form of live **entertainment** that Alex likes is plays. There are several theaters in his town. Last month, Alex saw two plays. The first one was a comedy. Alex thought the actors were very funny. The second one was a musical, and he thought everyone sang really well. Alex hopes to see more plays soon.

Alex wishes he could be an actor or a musician, but he doesn't have any **talent**. He has to be satisfied with watching other people perform.

Definitions

Write each word next to its definition.

band	downtown	hall	play
club	entertainment	orchestra	purchase
concert	film	performance	talent

_____ 1. a movie

_____ 2. a story that is performed by actors in a theater

_____ 3. a large group of musicians playing different kinds of instruments, and usually playing classical music

_____ 4. a large building where public events are held

_____ 5. a group of people who play music together, especially a group that plays rock or jazz music

_____ 6. an occasion on which some live entertainment is shown to an audience

_____ 7. a place for evening entertainment where there is usually music, dancing, food and drinks

_____ 8. something that amuses or interests people

_____ 9. to get something by paying money for it

_____ 10. a performance of music in front on an audience

_____ 11. in the main business area of a town or city

_____ 12. natural skill or ability

Abbreviations

Match each abbreviation with the
word(s) that it represents.

> The days of the week and times of day have
> abbreviations in English. When you read an abbreviation,
> you say the whole word. For example, when you read
> *Mon.*, you say *Monday.*

_____	1. Wed.	a.	Thursday
_____	2. a.m.	b.	weekend
_____	3. eve.	c.	ante meridiem (morning)
_____	4. wknd.	d.	Tuesday
_____	5. Tues.	e.	afternoon
_____	6. p.m.	f.	evening
_____	7. aft.	g.	Wednesday
_____	8. Thurs.	h.	post meridiem (afternoon & evening)

Exercise 3: Word Builder

Prefix

> The prefix *multi–* means *many.*

Choose a word from the box, add *multi–* to it, and write it on the line.

colored	family	media	national
cultural	lingual	millionaire	purpose

1. A _____ donated the money to build the concert hall.

2. It was a _____ performance, and I understood all of the languages.

3. They wore _____ costumes that contained red, blue, green, and yellow.

4. The school concerts are in the _____ room, where the children also eat lunch.

5. That is a _____ building, containing at least 10 apartments.

6. The orchestra is _____, with representatives from five countries.

7. It was a _____ show, with lights, recorded music, and live performances.

8. The _____ film festival showed movies from many cultures.

Suffixes

The suffix –*ment* changes a verb into a noun.

Study each rule. Then fill in the noun form of the verb in parentheses.

Rule: Add –*ment* to a verb to change it to a noun.
Example: develop + ment = development

1. (entertain)   A concert is a form of live _____.

2. (enjoy)   He plays an instrument for _____.

3. (agree)   We are in _____ about which movie to see.

4. (move)   The dancer's _____ is graceful.

5. (improve)   We noticed a big _____ after the rehearsal.

6. (require)   It is a _____.

The suffix –*ance* changes a verb into a noun.

Study each rule. Then fill in the noun form of the verb in parentheses.

Rule 1: If a verb ends with –*ant*, drop the –*t* and add –*ce*.
Example: significant + ce = significance

7. (important)   What is the _____ of that?

8. (tolerant)   The conductor has no _____ for mistakes.

9. (distant)   What is the _____ to the theater?

10. (elegant)   The _____ of the star amazed us.

Rule 2: Add –*ance* to verbs that do not end with –*t*.
Example: attend + ance = attendance

11. (perform)   When is the _____?

12. (attend)   _____ at rehearsals is important.

13. (disturb)   There was a _____ during the concert.

14. (appear)   The star made an _____ after the show.

15. (assist)   The bass player needed _____ with her instrument.

Synonyms

Look at each underlined word. Choose a word from the box with a similar meaning and write it on the line.

amuse	film	likes
buy	forms	talents

1. Alex <u>enjoys</u> films, but he _____ plays even more.

2. I don't usually like watching <u>movies</u>, but I loved the international _____ festival.

3. She has the <u>ability</u> to play the piano but no other _____.

4. Alex likes many _____ of live entertainment, but concerts are his favorite <u>type</u>.

5. Comedy shows <u>entertain</u> him, and some movies _____ him as well.

6. He wanted to _____ tickets for next week's show, but a sign said "No Advance <u>Purchases</u>."

Collocations

> English speakers use many collocations when talking about places they go for entertainment.

Choose a word from the box to complete each collocation below.

amusement	baseball	concert	movie
art	circus	game	night

1. The symphony orchestra played in the _____ hall.

2. He is a ticket taker in the _____ theater.

3. We saw two games at the _____ stadium.

4. I went on a dozen rides at the _____ park.

5. We used all of our quarters in the machines in the _____ room.

6. They danced to the jazz band in the _____ club.

7. We saw clowns and elephants in the _____ tent.

8. I saw some nice paintings at the _____ museum.

Confusing Words

In each of the following, circle the word
that best completes the sentence.

Hear and *listen* both have to do with using your ears.
Hear means *to use your ears in a natural way, without
thinking about it.* *Listen* means *to use the ears on
purpose.* If there is an object after the verb, *listen* is
followed by *to.*

1. I (heard/listened) to a recording of the concert.

2. I (heard/listened) someone talking in the audience.

3. We couldn't (hear/listen) some of the actors on the stage.

4. When we were walking out, I (heard/listened) some people talking about the movie.

5. (Hear/Listen)! The concert is about to begin.

6. Do you want to (hear/listen) to my new CD?

7. I can't (hear/listen) you. Can you speak louder?

8. Don't (hear/listen) to what he is saying.

In each of the following, write
amusing or *amused* on the line.

Amusing and *amused* are both adjectives. *Amusing*
describes the person or event that causes amusement.
Amused describes the person that feels the amusement.

9. We laughed at the _____ play.

10. The people in the audience were _____, so they laughed.

11. That _____ movie is still in the theaters.

12. I think he's a very _____ comedian. Everyone laughs at him.

13. At first we were _____, but in the end we didn't think it was funny.

14. I only like _____ TV shows. I don't like serious ones.

15. Some people thought the joke was funny, but I was not _____.

16. Clowns are usually _____, but some children are afraid of them.

Context Clues

Copy the two words or phrases with similar meanings in each of the following.

> When you guess from context, you can often find a word with a similar meaning in the same sentence. Look for words like *same, like, and, both,* and the verb *to be* to show that a sentence contains words with similar meanings.

1. Violins and violas are both stringed orchestra instruments.

   _____   _____

2. A concert hall is like a theater, since they both have seats, aisles, and a stage.

   _____   _____

3. We enjoyed all of the entertainers and performers in the show.

   _____   _____

4. I only like foreign films, and my sister only likes adventure movies.

   _____   _____

5. The high school play was on Friday, and the middle school production was on Saturday.

   _____   _____

6. On their vacation, they visited all of the art museums and galleries.

   _____   _____

7. You play a piccolo the same way you play a flute.

   _____   _____

8. At the circus, the clown amused the children and the acrobats entertained the adults.

   _____   _____

9. The same musician who conducts the orchestra also directs the chorus.

   _____   _____

10. The dance scene in the play was like a ballet I once saw.

    _____   _____

11. Alex enjoys all kinds of movies, and he likes live performances as well.

    _____   _____

12. He likes all forms of entertainment, but live performances are his favorite type.

    _____   _____

Parts of Speech

Identify the underlined words. Write *N*
on the line if the word is a noun, and
write *V* if it is a verb.

> **Many common vocabulary words can work either as
> nouns or as verbs. Look for a noun after a possessive or
> possessive adjective. Look for a verb after a subject
> or after *to*.**

_____ 1. I saw the Italian director's new <u>film</u> last weekend.

_____ 2. Do you know how to <u>dance</u>?

_____ 3. That actor <u>plays</u> a doctor on TV.

_____ 4. Alex <u>purchases</u> tickets as soon as he can.

_____ 5. She knows how to <u>play</u> the saxophone.

_____ 6. I went to see my little sister's <u>play</u> in her high school.

_____ 7. They <u>film</u> a lot of movies in New York.

_____ 8. You need to keep the receipt for your <u>purchases</u>.

_____ 9. I enjoyed the ballerina's final <u>dance</u>.

_____ 10. Do you have enough money to <u>purchase</u> them now?

Dictionary

Identify the part of speech of each underlined word. Write *N* or *V* on the line.
Then look up the word in your dictionary. Choose and write the best definition.

_____ 1. After the show, I couldn't wait to get my <u>film</u> developed to see the pictures.

definition: _____

_____ 2. I liked the first <u>act</u> of the play a lot better than the second.

definition: _____

_____ 3. They are going to hold the <u>dance</u> in the school gym.

definition: _____

_____ 4. What part does he <u>play</u> in the movie?

definition: _____

_____ 5. I want to <u>program</u> my VCR to record the movie.

definition: _____

Crossword Puzzle

Fill in the puzzle with words from the box.

Aft.	baseball	improvement	plays
amusing	club	listen	talented
appearance	entertainment	multimedia	tent
art	hall	orchestra	Wed.

ACROSS

3. Can I _____ to your CD?
5. All of the musicians in the band are _____.
7. Alex heard a jazz band in a night _____.
8. _____ is the abbreviation for *Wednesday.*
9. The clowns work in the circus _____.
10. The orchestra plays in the concert _____.
11. They got better. I noticed the _____.
12. He became famous after his _____ on TV.
15. I saw some great paintings in the _____ gallery.
16. He plays violin in the _____.

DOWN

1. The _____ production used sound and lights.
2. They play _____ in the stadium.
4. What do you like to do for _____?
6. The comedy show was _____.
13. Alex saw three _____ on Broadway last year.
14. _____ is the abbreviation for *afternoon.*

Vocabulary in Context

Choose a word from the box and write it on the line.

band	concert	film	performance	play

Alex had a busy weekend. On Friday night, he heard his favorite rock _____

1

play. Then on Saturday afternoon he attended the opening day of the international

_____ festival. On Saturday night he went to a _____

2   3

by the symphony orchestra, and on Sunday afternoon he went to a matinee

_____ of a new _____.

4   5

club	hall	museum	park	stadium	theater

We had a great time on our vacation. We went to two concerts. We heard a symphony in a

concert _____ and we heard a jazz band in a night _____. We

6   7

spent two days at local tourist attractions. One day we went to the art _____,

8

and another day we went to an amusement _____. We spent one rainy after-

9

noon in a movie _____. On the last day we saw a professional ball game at

10

the baseball _____. That was the best part of our vacation.

11

Multicultural	multilingual	multinational	multipurpose

Last Wednesday, Alex went to an event at his local school. They held the event in the

_____ room, a large room used for many activities. The event was

12

" _____ Night," showcasing all of the cultures in the school. One presentation

13

was _____. It was in several languages. The best presentation was a

14

_____ one. The students represented several countries.

15

Cars

In this lesson, you will work with words about cars. Read this description of what you should look at before you buy a used car.

If you are thinking about buying a used car, you should check the car carefully. First, look over the outside of the car. Are there any scratches on the **fenders** or the **bumpers?** Does it have all four **hubcaps?** Then open the **trunk**. Is it clean and dry? Next, take a look under the **hood**. You will probably want a mechanic to look at the engine, the battery, and the **transmission**, but you can see if it looks clean under the hood.

Next, you should get into the car. Sit in the driver's seat. Put your hands on the steering wheel. Do you feel comfortable? Put your feet on the **pedals**. Can you reach the gas pedal and the brake pedal easily? If the car has a standard transmission, can you reach the **clutch** easily? Are the gauges, instruments, and controls on the **dashboard** easy to read? Try the seatbelt on. Does it fit properly? Try looking out the **windshield**. Then try the mirrors. Look out both the rear view and the side view mirrors. If you can't see clearly out of the mirrors, the car might not be safe to drive.

After you decide whether you feel comfortable in the driver's seat, look around the interior of the car. How is the **upholstery?** Is it in good condition? Look at the back seat as well. Then look at the floors. Is the carpet worn, or is it in good condition?

Now it's time to turn the car on. Put the key in the **ignition** and turn it. Does it start easily? Then, turn on the headlights to see if they work, even if it is daytime. Turn on the windshield wipers, even if it's not raining. Try out the horn and the turn signals. Step on the brake pedal and have someone tell you if the brake lights are working.

If everything checks out with your inspection, it's time to drive the car. If you like the way it drives, this may be the car for you!

Definitions

Write each word next to its definition.

bumper	fenders	ignition	trunk
clutch	hood	pedal	upholstery
dashboard	hubcap	transmission	windshield

_____ 1. a part in a car or on a machine that you push with your foot in order to control something

_____ 2. a large area in the back of a car that is used to carry or store things like luggage, bags, or tools

_____ 3. the large piece of glass that you look through when driving a car

_____ 4. the pedal that you press before you change gears in a car with a standard transmission

_____ 5. the cloth or leather covering on car seats

_____ 6. the front panel in a car that contains gauges for speed and other information, controls for heating and cooling, and other instruments

_____ 7. the part of a car that takes power from the engine and sends it to the wheels

_____ 8. the sides of a car that are above and over the wheels

_____ 9. the metal lid that covers a car's engine

_____ 10. the heavy bar on the front or back of a vehicle to protect it if it hits something

_____ 11. a round metal cover over the center of a wheel on a car

_____ 12. the place in the car where you insert and turn a key in order to start the engine

Initializations

Match each initialization with what it stands for.

Initializations are a short form of two or more words. You can explain these initializations with sentences using *stands for.*

_____	1. EPA	a. miles per gallon
_____	2. mpg	b. General Motors
_____	3. AC	c. Environmental Protection Agency
_____	4. mph	d. miles per hour
_____	5. rpm	e. Department of Motor Vehicles
_____	6. SUV	f. revolutions per minute
_____	7. DMV	g. Air Conditioning
_____	8. GM	h. Sport Utility Vehicle

Exercise 3: Word Builder

Prefix

Choose a word from the box, add *pre–* to it, and write it on the line.

The prefix *pre-* means *before.* You can add *pre–* to some nouns, verbs, and adjectives.

arrange	fabricated	pay	test
caution	owned	teen	view

1. A _____ can't drive, but many teenagers can.

2. Wear your seatbelt as a _____, even though you probably won't have an accident.

3. You can _____ a car loan before you buy.

4. You can _____ your insurance premiums several months in advance.

5. You can _____ next year's models at the car show.

6. All of the parts are _____ in one factory and shipped to another.

7. Some people call used cars "_____."

8. If you take the _____, you'll know how much to study for your driving test.

Suffixes

> The suffix *–ship* indicates that a word is a noun that refers to a state or condition.

Study the rule. Then add *–ship* to the word in parentheses and write it on the line.

> **Rule: Add *–ship* to nouns to indicate a state or condition.**
> **Example: partner + ship = partnership**

1. (relation)   I have a good _____ with my mechanic.

2. (owner)   Car _____ is a big responsibility.

3. (member)   He has a _____ in the car club.

4. (champion)   That driver won the _____.

5. (partner)   The two car dealers have a _____.

Study each rule. Then write the noun form of the adjective in parentheses on the line.

> The suffix *–ity* is used to change an adjective into a noun.

> **Rule 1: If a word ends in *–ble*, drop the *–le* and add *–llIty*.**
> **Example: flexible + ity = flexibility**

6. (stable)   There are problems with _____ in some SUVs.

7. (able)   Do you have the _____ to drive a truck?

8. (possible)   If you need a car, leasing one is always a _____.

> **Rule 2: If a word ends in *–e*, drop the *–e* and add *–ity*.**
> **Example: active + ity = activity**

9. (intense)   The car salesman spoke with great _____.

10. (creative)   Car designers show a lot of _____.

> **Rule 3: If a word ends in a consonant, add *–ity*.**
> **Example: valid + ity = validity**

11. (real)   Car ownership can be a _____ for you.

12. (prior)   Paying for gas is a top _____.

13. (popular)   Hybrid cars are increasing in _____.

Synonyms

Look at each underlined word. Choose a word from the box with a similar meaning and write it on the line.

> | accelerate | gas pedal | parking brake |
> | brake | honk the horn | steer |

1. Set your _____ when you stop. This <u>emergency brake</u> will keep the car from rolling.

2. Use the wheel to _____ the car, but don't <u>turn</u> it too fast.

3. You should <u>slow down</u> or _____ before you get to the stop sign.

4. Take your foot off the <u>accelerator</u>—the _____—when you want to slow down.

5. When you begin to enter the highway you should <u>speed up</u>, or _____.

6. You can _____ in an emergency, but don't <u>blow the horn</u> just for fun.

Collocations

Choose a word from the box and write it on the line.

> There are a lot of prepositions that can be used when talking about cars.

> | down | in | on | up |

1. If you go too far, you can just back _____.

2. Before you come to the stop sign, you should slow _____.

3. Speed _____ before you merge onto the highway.

4. The mechanic is working _____ the transmission.

5. After you get _____ the car, put the key _____ the ignition.

6. Turn your headlights _____ when it gets dark.

7. When you see "Buckle _____!" that means to put your seatbelt _____.

8. You have to step _____ the gas pedal to make the car go.

Confusing Words

In each of the following, circle the word that best completes the sentence.

Invent and *discover* both have to do with new things. *Invent* means *to make something that did not exist before.* You can invent a machine or a process. *Discover* means *to find or see something that existed before but was not known.* You can discover a place, a thing, or a fact. *Invent* can only be used before nouns, but *discover* can be used before nouns or noun clauses *(ie. discovered that . . .).*

1. Before the (invention/discovery) of the CD player, most cars had cassette players.

2. Do you know who (invented/discovered) the automatic transmission?

3. Researchers have (invented/discovered) that airbags save lives.

4. Oil was (invented/discovered) in Pennsylvania in the 1800s.

5. Who (invented/discovered) the process for turning crude oil into gasoline?

6. After the (invention/discovery) of seat belts, cars became safer.

7. Benjamin Franklin (invented/discovered) that lightning was electricity.

8. Which (invention/discovery) is more important: the light bulb or the telephone?

9. I'm glad I (invented/discovered) the problem before I bought the car.

In each of the following, write *brake* or *break* on the line.

Brake and *break* sound the same but have different meanings. They can both be nouns or verbs. *Brake* has to do with stopping a car. *Break* can be about taking a rest, or it can have to do with damaging something.

10. You should _____ as soon as the light turns yellow.

11. If you _____ the windshield you can't drive the car.

12. Use your parking _____ on a hill.

13. We've worked a long time. Let's take a _____.

14. If we finish this, we can _____ for lunch.

15. He stepped on the _____ but couldn't stop the car in time.

16. I waited for a _____ in the traffic before I turned.

17. A lot of drivers _____ when they see a police car.

Context Clues

Circle the word or phrase that appears
right before the dash. Then underline or highlight the definition or defining
examples. Write *definition* or *examples* on the line.

In each of the following, a word or phrase is defined in
the context of the sentence. A definition or defining
examples appear after a dash.

_____ 1. I discovered that my car's battery—the device that makes
electricity by using chemical reactions—was dead.

_____ 2. Be sure your car's safety equipment—seatbelts, airbags—is in
good working order.

_____ 3. It's not a good idea to drive with a broken speedometer—the
instrument that tells you how fast you are driving.

_____ 4. You have to pay extra for optional equipment—a sunroof, power
windows, cruise control.

_____ 5. I think my brake lights—the red lights on the rear of my car that
get bright when I apply the brakes—are burned out.

_____ 6. Don't accelerate—speed up—when the light turns yellow.

_____ 7. You don't have to pay extra for standard equipment—a steering
wheel, a heater.

_____ 8. How much can you put in your trunk—the compartment at the
rear of the car for storing or carrying things?

_____ 9. Be sure that all of your passengers—the people riding with you
who are not driving—are wearing seatbelts.

_____ 10. You won't be able to fix a broken axle—the shaft on which the
car's wheels rotate.

_____ 11. You can get tickets for traffic violations—speeding, running a red
light.

_____ 12. Who put so many entertainment systems—a radio, CDs, tape
players, DVDs—into a car?

_____ 13. Is the odometer—the instrument that records the distance
traveled—broken?

_____ 14. Is a sedan—a car with two or four doors and a front and back
seat—the best kind of car to buy?

Parts of Speech

Identify the underlined words. Write *Adj.*
on the line if the word is an adjective,
and write *Adv.* if it is an adverb.

> Adjectives modify nouns, and adverbs usually modify
> action verbs. You can usually make an adverb from an
> adjective by adding *–ly,* but some words use the same
> word for both forms. Three of them are *fast, hard,* and
> *straight.* Look for an adjective before a noun or after *be.*
> Look for an adverb after an action verb.

_____ 1. She loves to go <u>fast</u>.

_____ 2. To get to the theater, drive <u>straight</u> down Main Street.

_____ 3. I like driving on <u>straight</u> roads.

_____ 4. It is <u>hard</u> to learn how to drive.

_____ 5. That is a <u>fast</u> car.

_____ 6. That mechanic worked <u>hard</u> on my car.

_____ 7. Is that road <u>straight</u>?

_____ 8. Driving a standard transmission is <u>hard</u>.

_____ 9. He was driving too <u>fast</u>.

_____ 10. She drove <u>straight</u> to the gas station.

Dictionary

Identify the part of speech of each underlined word. Write *N* or *V* on the line.
Then look up the word in your dictionary. Choose and write the best definition.

_____ 1. That car runs well, but the <u>body</u> is in poor condition.

definition: _____

_____ 2. You can't <u>pass</u> on that one-lane road.

definition: _____

_____ 3. You have to put the car in <u>gear</u> before it will go.

definition: _____

_____ 4. I <u>park</u> my car in front of my house.

definition: _____

_____ 5. My car has four new <u>tires</u>.

definition: _____

Crossword Puzzle

Fill in the puzzle with words from the box.

AC	down	ignition	possibility	trunk
accelerate	GM	Mpg	preview	up
brake	honk	on	safety	windshield
bumper	hubcaps	ownership	steer	

ACROSS

2. Car _____ is a big responsibility.
6. We can put the suitcases in the _____.
8. I backed my car into a tree and scratched the _____.
10. _____ stands for General Motors.
11. Don't forget to buckle _____.
14. You should _____ when you enter the highway.
16. Put the parking _____ on when you stop.
18. Slow _____ when the light turns yellow.
19. Keep both hands on the wheel when you _____ the car.

DOWN

1. _____ stands for *miles per gallon.*
3. I usually clean my _____ at the gas station.
4. Don't _____ your horn here.
5. When cars hit potholes, sometimes their _____ fall off.
7. First, put the key in the _____.
9. If the car won't start, one _____ is a dead battery.
12. At the car show, you can _____ next year's models.
13. I worry about the _____ of a car without airbags.
15. Put your headlights _____ at night.
17. _____ stands for *air conditioning.*

Vocabulary in Context

Choose a word from the box and write it on the line.

| dashboard | hood | pedals | upholstery |

Before you buy your car, sit in it to be sure it is comfortable. Can you see and reach all of the instruments on the _____? How about the _____? Are your
1   2

legs long enough to reach them comfortably? Can you look over the _____
3

and see the road in front of you? Finally, pay attention to the _____. If it is
4

plastic, the seats might get too hot in the summer.

| prearrange | precautions | prepay | pretest | preview |

I am going to take the test to get my driver's license. I want to _____
5

everything so there will be no surprises. First, I know that I can _____ some
6

of the questions from the test on the Internet. I think I can even take a _____
7

for practice. Then, I am going to _____ the fee online, so I won't have any
8

trouble at the DMV. I'm taking a lot of _____ because I want to pass the test
9

the first time I take it.

| down | in | on | up |

I'm going to tell you how to drive a car. First, get _____ the car. Put the key
10

_____ the ignition and turn the car _____. If it is hot, the next
11   12

thing you should do is put _____ the windows. Now, you are almost ready to
13

drive, but don't forget to buckle _____! When you are ready to move forward,
14

press _____ the accelerator to go. Keep your hands _____
15   16

the steering wheel and your eyes _____ the road at all times!
17

Health Care

In this lesson, you will work with words about health and health care. Read this story about a family's health problems.

It's been a month full of health problems in Marian's house. It seems that everyone has had a problem! First, Marian's husband Ted got sick. He had a **fever** and a sore throat. He stayed in bed for two days. Then, he made an appointment with his **physician**. When he arrived in the doctor's office, the nurse checked his temperature and took his blood pressure. The doctor thought that Ted had an **infection**. So the doctor did a test. He wanted to find out if it was a viral infection or one caused by bacteria. The results showed that it was a **bacterial** infection. The doctor gave Ted a **prescription** for antibiotics. Ted took the medicine. He felt better in a few days.

Next, Marian's son Tom had a little accident. He fell while he was riding his bicycle. Immediately, his wrist **swelled**. Marian took him right away to the emergency room of the hospital. She was afraid that it was a **fracture**. The doctor took some x-rays. Then he told Marian and Tom that the wrist was only **sprained**. The doctor put Tom's arm in a sling and Tom left the hospital a short time later. Marian is going to have the **pediatrician** check the wrist in about a week. Tom feels much better now.

It was the dog's turn next. Fluffy, the family dog, was coughing and sneezing. He was sleeping a lot. His nose was warm and dry. He didn't want to play with his toys. Marian took Fluffy to the vet **clinic**. The **veterinarian** gave Marian some tablets to give to Fluffy. Fluffy feels better now, too.

Finally, Marian was feeling very tired. She went to see her doctor. The doctor did some blood tests and discovered that Marian is **anemic**. She started to take iron pills. Now she is starting to feel better. She hopes everyone stays healthy for a while.

Definitions

Write each word next to its definition.

anemic	fever	pediatrician	sprain
bacteria	fracture	physician	swell
clinic	infection	prescription	veterinarian

_____ 1. a break or crack, often in a bone

_____ 2. to damage a joint by twisting or stretching it suddenly

_____ 3. very small living things; some of them cause diseases

_____ 4. a doctor who takes care of children

_____ 5. to increase in size because of an injury

_____ 6. a doctor of medicine; a more formal way of saying doctor

_____ 7. a place where people receive medical treatment, especially if they do not need to stay in a hospital

_____ 8. a piece of paper written by a doctor that a patient takes to a pharmacy to get medicine

_____ 9. suffering from a condition in which there are too few oxygen-carrying red blood cells in your blood

_____ 10. a doctor who is trained to give medical care to animals

_____ 11. a body temperature that is higher than normal, usually caused by an illness

_____ 12. a disease caused by germs such as bacteria or viruses

Initializations

Match each initialization with what it stands for.

Initializations are a short form of one or more words. You can explain these initializations with sentences using *stands for*.

_____ 1. M.D. a. Emergency Room

_____ 2. OR b. Licensed Practical Nurse

_____ 3. ER c. Registered Nurse

_____ 4. RN d. Cardiopulmonary Resuscitation

_____ 5. CPR e. Doctor of Medicine

_____ 6. ICU f. Intravenous

_____ 7. LPN g. Magnetic Resonance Imaging

_____ 8. IV h. Operating Room

_____ 9. MRI i. Intensive Care Unit

Exercise 3: Word Builder

Prefix

Choose a word from the box, add *over–* to it, and write it on the line.

The prefix *over–* means *excessive* or *too much.* You can add *over–* to some verbs and adjectives.

charged	crowded	estimated	priced	worked
cook	eat	flow	ruled	

1. If you _____, you will gain weight.

2. The ER was _____. The patients were in the hallways.

3. I hear that many doctors are _____ when they are in training.

4. He _____ my recovery time. He said it would be six weeks and it was four.

5. I think the hospital _____ me. The bill was for too much money.

6. The vitamins in that store are _____. I buy less expensive ones.

7. Vegetables are better for you if you don't _____ them.

8. If you put any more water in that glass, it will _____.

9. My doctor wanted to operate, but he was _____ by the other doctors.

Suffixes

> The suffix –*ist* indicates that a word refers to a person who is trained or skilled in an area.

Study each rule. Then add –*ist* to the word in parentheses and write it on the line.

> **Rule 1: If a noun ends in –*y*, drop the –*y* and add –*ist*.**
> **Example: pharmacy + ist = pharmacist**

1. (biology)   A _____ discovered that virus.

2. (psychology)   I had an appointment with a _____.

3. (zoology)   A _____ worked with the veterinarian.

4. (technology)   The _____ works in the MRI lab.

5. (therapy)   She saw a _____ when she was recovering.

> **Rule 2: Add –*ist* to nouns that end with consonants.**
> **Example: art + Ist = artist**

6. (journal)   The _____ wrote about the problems.

7. (art)   They hired an _____ to paint a mural in the pediatric wing.

8. (reception)   The _____ made the appointment.

> The suffix –*ian* also indicates that a person has a skill in an area.

Study the rule. Then add –*ian* to the word in parentheses and write it on the line. Note the pronunciation change.

> **Rule: Add –*ian* to adjectives and nouns that end in –*ic*.**
> **Example: clinic + ian = clinician**

9. (pediatric)   She took the child to a _____.

10. (optic)   The _____ made his glasses.

11. (diagnostic)   That doctor is a good _____.

12. (mathematic)   The _____ figured out the formula.

Antonyms

Choose an antonym from the box for each underlined word and write
it on the line.

awake	**elderly**	**heat**	**well**
discharged	**energetic**	**overweight**	**worried**

1. Being <u>underweight</u> can be just as unhealthy as being _____.

2. You should apply <u>cold</u> compresses to some injuries and _____ to others.

3. The doctor seemed <u>unconcerned</u>, but the patient's family was _____.

4. A gerontologist deals with _____ people, and a pediatrician works with <u>young</u> people.

5. He was <u>tired and sluggish</u> when he was sick, but now he's more _____.

6. The patient was <u>admitted to</u> the hospital on Monday and _____ on Friday.

7. The patient was <u>asleep</u> when the doctor came, but he was _____ later.

8. He was <u>sick</u> for a long time, but now he's quite _____.

Collocations

English has many collocations that describe people who work in the health care field.

Choose a word from the box to complete
each collocation below.

administrator	**emergency**	**specialist**	**therapist**
aide	**hygienist**	**technician**	

1. The x-ray _____ took the patient to radiology.

2. He is going to school to be a dental _____.

3. She is a cardiac _____.

4. He spoke to the hospital _____ about his problem.

5. She went to a physical _____ for treatment.

6. She works as a nurse's _____ in a nursing home.

7. The _____ medical technician came in the ambulance.

Confusing Words

In each of the following, write *affect(s)*
or *effect(s)* on the line.

> *Affect* and *effect* sound alike but work differently. *Affect*
> is a verb that means *to have an influence on something.*
> *Effect* is a noun that is the result of the influence.

1. How did the medicine _____ you?

2. What are the _____ of being overweight?

3. Can being underweight _____ your health?

4. The medicine _____ everyone differently.

5. She's worried about the negative _____ of smoking.

6. Most people don't experience any side-_____ from those pills.

7. You have to take the positive _____ with the negative ones.

8. If that _____ you that way, stop taking it.

In each of the following, write *advice* or
advise on the line.

> *Advice* and *advise* are often confused. *Advice* is a noun
> that tells about an idea that someone gives you to help
> you. *Advise* is a verb that means *to give advice.*

9. The doctor gave me some good _____.

10. Did you take the _____?

11. I think I need to ask for _____.

12. He's going to _____ you to stop smoking.

13. Who will _____ me about this?

14. The _____ was good, but I didn't take it.

15. If your doctors _____ you to do it, then you should.

16. I can't _____ you on medical matters.

Context Clues

In each of the following, decide if the underlined words have close to the same meaning or close to the opposite meaning. Write *same* or *opposite* on the line.

_____ 1. The old man told the doctor all about his <u>aches</u> and <u>pains</u>.

_____ 2. The vet wanted her to give her cat one <u>tablet</u> per day, but have you ever tried to give a <u>pill</u> to a cat?

_____ 3. Some elderly people can be very <u>feeble</u>, but my grandfather is really <u>strong</u>.

_____ 4. The patient was very <u>ill</u> last week, but this week he seems rather <u>healthy</u>.

_____ 5. You need to wash the <u>germs</u> off your hands, since <u>bacteria</u> cause illness.

_____ 6. Tom had a <u>mild</u> case of the flu, but his brother Bob had a <u>severe</u> case and was much sicker.

_____ 7. Some of the tests came back <u>positive</u>, but the good news is that the important ones came back <u>negative</u>.

_____ 8. The rash <u>appeared</u> on her arm, but then it <u>vanished</u>.

_____ 9. The doctor called for an <u>assistant</u>, and an <u>aide</u> came in right away.

_____ 10. The form asked for a <u>spouse's</u> name, so Marian wrote her <u>husband's</u> name.

_____ 11. You should see a <u>doctor</u> about that problem because only <u>physicians</u> can write prescriptions.

_____ 12. Patients who can't eat <u>solid</u> food have to have a <u>liquid</u> diet.

_____ 13. I <u>slipped</u> on the ice, and when I <u>slid</u> I sprained my ankle.

_____ 14. She <u>fractured</u> her wrist last year, and it was a terrible experience since she'd never <u>broken</u> a bone before.

_____ 15. Good <u>nutrition</u> can keep you healthy, so be careful of your <u>diet</u>.

Parts of Speech

Identify the underlined words. Write *V* on
the line if the word is a verb, and write *Adj.* if it is an adjective.

> Many common vocabulary words that end in *–ed* can work either as verbs or as adjectives. Look for a verb after a subject. Look for an adjective before a noun.

_____ 1. Ned <u>fractured</u> his arm when he was a child.

_____ 2. I get nervous in <u>crowded</u> places.

_____ 3. A <u>sprained</u> wrist can be very uncomfortable.

_____ 4. A <u>fractured</u> bone takes several weeks to heal.

_____ 5. The accident <u>injured</u> all of the people in the car.

_____ 6. I <u>sprained</u> my ankle when I was ice skating.

_____ 7. More than a dozen people <u>crowded</u> into the tiny office.

_____ 8. They took the <u>injured</u> people away by ambulance.

_____ 9. You can't dance on a <u>sprained</u> ankle.

_____ 10. The doctor put a splint on the <u>fractured</u> bone.

Dictionary

Identify the part of speech of each underlined word. Write *N* or *V* on
the line. Then look up the word in your dictionary. Choose and write
the best definition.

_____ 1. I need to go to the doctor and have a <u>physical</u>.

definition: _____

_____ 2. Did she <u>nurse</u> the sick dog back to health?

definition: _____

_____ 3. He couldn't swallow the <u>tablet</u>, so he got the liquid medicine.

definition: _____

_____ 4. All of my muscles <u>ache</u> after the exercise.

definition: _____

_____ 5. The doctor gave him a <u>sling</u> after he sprained his wrist.

definition: _____

Crossword Puzzle

Fill in the puzzle with words from the box.

anemic	fever	overweight	tablet
effects	optician	receptionist	therapist
energetic	overcharge	RN	veterinarian
ER	overeat	swell	well

ACROSS

1. Another word for pill is _____.
4. _____ stands for *emergency room*.
6. If you _____ you will gain weight.
8. If you don't put ice on the injury, it will _____ up.
9. Check your hospital bill carefully to make sure they didn't _____ you.
11. The _____ answers the phone in the doctor's office.
13. If you are _____, you might have health problems.

DOWN

2. The drug has some bad side-_____.
3. The _____ took care of my dog.
4. The opposite of tired or sluggish is _____.
5. If you don't have enough red blood cells, then you are _____.
7. She went to a physical _____ after her accident.
9. An _____ made my glasses.
10. An elevated temperature is a _____.
11. _____ stands for *registered nurse*.
12. The opposite of sick is _____.

Vocabulary in Context

Choose a word from the box and write it on the line.

advised	fractured	infection	pediatrician	sprained

Marian's son Tom has been to the _____ several times this year. First, he had

an _____ and the doctor gave him an antibiotic. Then he

2

_____ his wrist, and the doctor put it in a cast. After that he

3

_____ his ankle and the doctor _____ him not to walk for a

4   5

couple of days.

ER	ICU	IV	MRI	OR

Last year, my father was in the hospital. I got used to talking in initials. First, he went to the

_____—the emergency room. The technicians took some x-rays and did an _____. They

6   7

discovered that he needed surgery, so they took him to the _____ for the operation. Before

8

they operated, they inserted an _____ into a vein to give him drugs intravenously. The surgery

9

went well, but he was in the _____ for several days afterwards.

10

overcharged	overcooked	overcrowded	overpriced	overworked

Everyone at the hospital is complaining. The doctors are complaining because they are

_____. The nurses in the ER are complaining about the _____

11   12

waiting room. The patient in the billing office is complaining about being

_____. The visitors in the cafeteria are complaining that the food is both

13

_____ and _____.

14   15

Banking

In this lesson, you will work with words about banks and banking. Read this description of the services offered by a bank.

Welcome to Sun Star Bank. We are a full-service bank ready to help with all of your banking needs. We can help manage your money with our convenient checking accounts. Don't keep a lot of **cash** in your house. Instead, let us keep it for you. If you **deposit** your money with us, you can **withdraw** cash conveniently at our ATMs. Or you can write a **check** for the amount that you need.

If you want to save money, we can also help you with that. You can open a passbook **savings** account. If you deposit a little each week, soon your account will have a lot of money in it. Your money will earn **interest**, too. Visit one of our branches to find out what our current interest rate is. You can't access your savings account through the ATM, but you can easily withdraw money in the bank. Just bring in your account number and some identification. We'll also give you a **passbook** to keep track of how much money you have in the account.

If plastic is what you need, we can give you a **debit** card or a **credit** card. You can use them at many stores. When you use the debit card, the money comes right out of your checking account. Be sure to memorize your PIN—your personal identification number—because you'll need it every time you use the card. Or if you prefer, you can apply for one of our credit cards. You have to pay interest on the money that you **charge** on your credit card.

If you need more money than you can charge on your credit card, we can give you a **loan**. Visit a loan officer to find out if you qualify for one. Most of our loans can be paid back over five years, and we don't have a penalty if you pay off the loan early. Sun Star Bank is the flexible answer to all of your **financial** needs!

Definitions

Write each word next to its definition.

cash	credit	financial	passbook
charge	debit	interest	savings
check	deposit	loan	withdraw

_____ 1. a book in which you keep a record of money that is added to or taken out of a savings account

_____ 2. having to do with money or managing money

_____ 3. a printed paper that you write an amount of money on and sign in order to get money from an account

_____ 4. an amount of money that you borrow from a bank or other institution

_____ 5. to pay for something with a credit card

_____ 6. an amount of money taken out of an account

_____ 7. to put into a bank account

_____ 8. money that is paid for the use of another person's money

_____ 9. money that is in the form of bills or coins

_____ 10. an amount of money that a person saves

_____ 11. to take money out of a bank account

_____ 12. an arrangement with a bank or store that allows you to buy something now and pay for it later

Initializations

Match each initialization with what it stands for.

Initializations are a short form of one or more words. You can explain these initializations with sentences using *stands for.*

_____ 1. PIN (pronounced /*pin*/)

_____ 2. CD

_____ 3. ATM

_____ 4. APR

_____ 5. FDIC

_____ 6. ID

_____ 7. COD

_____ 8. SSN

a. Automatic (automated) Teller Machine

b. Social Security Number

c. Cash on Delivery

d. Federal Deposit Insurance Corporation

e. Personal Identification Number

f. Annual Percentage Rate

g. Identification

h. Certificate of Deposit

Exercise 3: Word Builder

Prefix

The prefix *mis–* means *badly* when it is added to a verb.

Choose a word from the box, add *mis–* to it, and write it on the line.

calculated	informed	pronounces
counted	managed	spelled
directed	placed	understood

1. The teller always greets me, but she always _____ my name.

2. I _____ my checkbook so I can't pay by check.

3. The teller _____ me. He thought I said I wanted to withdraw a million dollars.

4. Please tell me the right information. I don't want to be _____.

5. The manager was fired because he _____ the bank.

6. I was sent to the wrong department four times. I don't want to be _____ again.

7. The teller _____ the money and had to count it again.

8. I was upset when I got my new checks because the printer _____ my name.

9. The bank _____ my interest, and I paid too much on my loan.

Suffix

The suffix –al indicates that a word is a noun. You can add –al to some verbs to change them into nouns.

Study each rule. Then add –al to the word in parentheses and write it on the line.

Rule 1: If a word ends in –e, drop the –e and add –al.
Example: propose + al = proposal

1. (refuse)   I was surprised by his _____.

2. (arrive)   What time is the _____?

3. (appraise)   They needed an _____ of the car's value.

4. (survive)   I read about his _____.

5. (propose)   The loan officer wrote a _____.

Rule 2: If a word ends in consonant and –y, change the –y to –i
and add –al.
Example: bury + al = burial

6. (bury)   We attended the _____ at the cemetery.

7. (deny)   He denied stealing, but I didn't hear his _____.

8. (try)   They showed a lot of evidence at the _____.

Rule 3: Add –al to all other verbs.
Example: dismiss + al = dismissal

9. (withdraw)   I want to make a _____ at the bank.

10. (dismiss)   Three o'clock is the school's _____ time.

11. (portray)   The actor's _____ was very good.

12. (betray)   The criminal's _____ of his partner helped the police.

Antonyms

Choose an antonym from the box for each underlined word and write it on the line.

borrow	deposited	high	penalty
careful	fake	outside	spend

1. Yesterday I _____ $500 in the bank, but today I had to <u>withdraw</u> half of it.

2. Don't _____ money from the bank! I can <u>lend</u> you some money.

3. If you don't _____ all of your paycheck, you can <u>save</u> some of it in the bank.

4. Interest rates were very _____ last year, but now they are <u>low</u>.

5. You can make a withdrawal _____ at the drive-in window, or <u>inside</u> at the counter.

6. That check is _____! If it were <u>real</u> it would have a design on the back.

7. There is a _____ if you don't pay on time, but no <u>reward</u> for paying early.

8. Tellers have to be _____. <u>Careless</u> tellers are often fired.

Collocations

Many collocations involve the word *pay*.

Choose a word from the box to complete each collocation below.

attention	for	to	visit
back	off	up	

1. If you lend me a dollar I'll pay you _____ tomorrow.

2. Hard work always pays _____ in the end.

3. I need to pay a _____ to my grandmother.

4. After I pay _____ my loans I'll feel better.

5. I think it really pays _____ save a little each week.

6. How much did you pay _____ those shoes?

7. I need the money back right now! Pay _____!

8. The guard pays _____ to everything in the bank.

Confusing Words

In each of the following, circle the word that best completes the sentence.

Borrow and *lend* both have to do with one person using another's money or things. When you *borrow* something or some money, you take it and promise to return it. When you *lend* something or some money, you let a person use it but you expect it to be returned.

1. I went to the bank because I needed to (borrow/lend) money to buy a car.

2. The bank (borrowed/lent) me the money for my tuition.

3. Can I (borrow/lend) your dictionary?

4. I need to (borrow/lend) a car to drive to the job interview.

5. If I (borrow/lend) you this today, will you return it tomorrow?

6. If you can't afford to lose that money, then don't (borrow/lend) it to anyone.

7. If you let me (borrow/lend) 10 dollars, I promise to pay you back next week.

8. I don't usually like to (borrow/lend) money if I am not sure that I can pay it back.

In each of the following, write *there* or *their* on the line.

There and *their* sound the same, so they are often confused in writing. *There* can be an adverb that means *in a particular place,* and it can be a pronoun that is used to say that something exists. *Their* is a possessive adjective that tells that something belongs to people.

9. I need to go to the bank because I haven't been _____ in a week.

10. _____ is a new bank right around the corner.

11. I like the tellers in my old bank because of _____ friendly smiles.

12. Some people never go into a bank. They use _____ ATM cards for everything.

13. If you need a pen to sign the check, _____ is one on the table.

14. What do banks do to keep _____ customers happy?

15. I know some people who use _____ debit cards for everything.

16. If you want to talk to the loan officer, he is over _____.

Context Clues

Circle the word or phrase that appears right before the dash. Then underline or highlight the definition or defining examples. Write *definition* or *examples* on the line.

In each of the following items, words are defined in the context of the sentence. A definition or defining examples appear after a dash.

_____ 1. The teller said she would debit—take money out of—my account.

_____ 2. I think he has some extra money to invest—to give to a company or bank in order to get a profit back.

_____ 3. Be sure to have all of your banking documents—checks, pass book, identification—before you come to the appointment.

_____ 4. I was 12 years old when I opened my first savings account—a bank account that pays interest.

_____ 5. How much money do you have in cash—coins and bills?

_____ 6. Try not to pay too many charges—interest, fees, penalties.

_____ 7. I need to find my checking account balance—the amount of money that I have in the account.

_____ 8. If you get that car loan, you will pay a lot of interest—money that you pay for borrowing money.

_____ 9. You can complete all of your transactions—deposits and withdrawals—here at the ATM.

_____ 10. If you want a home loan, you first have to get an appraisal—an official judgment of the value.

_____ 11. When you get your ATM card, you'll also get a personal identification number—a four-digit number that you have to type into the keypad when you use the ATM.

_____ 12. Personal loans can be used for home improvement—a new roof, a deck, or some renovations, for example.

Parts of Speech

Identify the underlined words. Write *N*
on the line if the word is a noun, and
write *V* if it is a verb.

> Many common vocabulary words can work either as
> nouns or as verbs. Look for a noun after a possessive.
> Look for a verb after *to*.

_____ 1. I need to charge it because I left my <u>cash</u> at home.

_____ 2. I can go online to <u>check</u> my balance.

_____ 3. The bank didn't record my <u>deposit</u>.

_____ 4. She needs to <u>balance</u> her checkbook.

_____ 5. The dress shop wouldn't accept my <u>check</u>.

_____ 6. I can call the bank to find out my <u>balance</u>.

_____ 7. When are you going to <u>deposit</u> the money?

_____ 8. When are you going to <u>cash</u> your check?

Dictionary

Identify the part of speech of each underlined word. Write *N* or *V* on
the line. Then look up the word in your dictionary. Choose and write
the best definition.

_____ 1. I need to <u>balance</u> my checkbook.

definition: _____

_____ 2. I made a big <u>deposit</u> into my savings account last week.

definition: _____

_____ 3. The bank overcharged me so they are going to <u>credit</u> my account.

definition: _____

_____ 4. I just got the <u>statement</u> for my account in the mail.

definition: _____

_____ 5. They keep the cash in the <u>safe</u>.

definition: _____

Crossword Puzzle

Fill in the puzzle with words from the box.

appraisal	borrow	invest	misunderstood	SSN
ATM	cash	lend	passbook	their
back	deposit	misdirected	PIN	There
balance	interest	misplaced	safe	withdraw

ACROSS

1. I am going to _____ money into my account.
3. You can withdraw cash from the _____.
6. I'll pay you _____ tomorrow.
10. What is the _____ rate on the loan?
12. He _____ my question.
13. The bank keeps cash in the _____.
15. I didn't lose my checkbook; I only _____ it.
16. I need to know my account _____.
18. I'm going to _____ some money from my account.

DOWN

2. You keep a record of how much money is in your savings account in a _____.
3. The bank will need an _____ of the value of your house.
4. _____ is a new bank on the corner.
5. I don't have money to _____.
6. I am going to _____ some money to pay for school.
7. I got paid and I need to _____ my check.
8. They _____ me and sent me to the wrong place.
9. _____ stands for *Social Security Number.*
11. They are very careful with _____ money.
14. I had to memorize my _____ for the ATM.
17. I hope you can _____ me some money.

Vocabulary in Context
Choose a word from the box and write it on the line.

CD	financial	invest	savings
checking	interest	loans	

Our bank can meet all of your _____ needs! We offer _____

accounts and passbook _____ accounts. You can _____

your money in a _____. If you need extra cash, we offer

_____ with a good _____ rate.

---

miscounted	misinformed	mismanaged	mispronounces	misspelled

I'm looking for a new bank because my old bank has a lot of problems. First, it is

_____. In fact, I think the manager never does anything. And the tellers are

terrible. One day, a teller _____ my money and gave me 100 dollars too

much. Another teller tries to call me by my name, but she _____ it every time.

And another teller _____ my name on my savings account, and that caused a

big problem. Finally, no one in the bank knows the correct information because everyone is

_____.

---

attention	back	for	off	to

You should pay _____ to your finances. My cousin did, and he is proof that it

really pays _____ do that. He took out some student loans to pay

_____ his education. He had to pay _____ the money when

he graduated. He made all of the payments on time, and in three years he had paid

_____ the loans. Now, he has his degree and doesn't owe anything, so he is

ready to buy a house!

Computers

In this lesson, you will work with words about computers. Read this story about how Mark bought a computer.

Last month, Mark realized that it was time to get a computer. He had been living without e-mail, Internet access, or a word processor up until then. He decided that he wanted to use all of those modern conveniences. First, Mark had to buy the **hardware** and **software**, and then he had to learn how to use the programs.

Mark found a computer store near his apartment. There, a sales associate helped him choose a computer. He got everything he needed. He got the CPU, the **monitor**, the keyboard, and a mouse. The computer came with a lot of **memory** and a CD/DVD **drive**. Mark also got a printer and a **scanner**. He was nervous about setting the computer up at home, but the instructions were clear.

The computer came with a lot of software already loaded. It had a word processing program, a **spreadsheet** program, and an Internet **browser**. It also had many other useful programs. There was only one problem with this. Mark didn't know how to use any of it. So he decided to take a course through his local adult education program. He took Introduction to Personal Computing. He learned everything he needed to know to get started.

The first thing the instructor taught Mark was how to start up the computer. He also learned how to shut it down. He learned the basics of his word processing program, like how to save **documents**. He learned how to do calculations with the spreadsheet program and how to get a free e-mail account through his Internet service provider. He learned how to **log on** to his e-mail and how to **log off.** The instructor also taught Mark how to check for computer **viruses** so that his computer won't **crash** unexpectedly from one.

Mark is very happy with his new computer and his new knowledge. He knows that he will use his new computer every day.

Definitions

Write each word or phrase next to its definition.

browser	drive	memory	software
crash	hardware	monitor	spreadsheet
document	log on	scanner	virus

_____ 1. a screen for a computer where information is displayed

_____ 2. to stop functioning suddenly because of a problem with the computer system

_____ 3. programs that operate a computer

_____ 4. a computer program that accesses and displays data on the Internet

_____ 5. a software program that can harm computer programs or files

_____ 6. a program that is used for accounting or bookkeeping that displays data in rows and columns

_____ 7. a device in a computer that is used to save and later read data

_____ 8. all of the parts of a computer that make it work, except for the programs

_____ 9. to enter a computer system or e-mail account, usually by typing a name and a password

_____ 10. the capacity that the computer has for storing data

_____ 11. a device that creates an image of a document or picture so that you can work with it on the computer

_____ 12. a piece of work created with a word processor

Exercise 2

Initializations

Match each initialization with what it stands for.

Initializations are a short form of one or more words. You can explain these initializations with sentences using *stands for.*

_____ 1. CPU

_____ 2. ROM (pronounced /rahm/)

_____ 3. HTML

_____ 4. WWW

_____ 5. ISP

_____ 6. PC

_____ 7. CD

_____ 8. http

_____ 9. DVD

a. Hypertext Transfer Protocol

b. Digital Versatile Disk

c. Read-only Memory

d. Central Processing Unit

e. Hypertext Markup Language

f. Compact Disk

g. Personal Computer

h. World Wide Web

i. Internet Service Provider

Exercise 3: Word Builder

Prefix

The prefix *un–* means *not* when it is added to an adjective.

Choose a word from the box, add *un–* to it, and write it on the line.

able	expected	necessary	readable
common	familiar	plugged	regulated

1. Before he took the class, Mark was _____ to even start up his computer.

2. The Internet is _____; anyone can post whatever they want.

3. He knows a lot about the word processor, but he is _____ with the spreadsheet.

4. He thought there was a problem with his printer, but it was only _____.

5. It's a good thing he knows how to type, since his handwriting is _____.

6. The computer crash was completely _____; we had no warning.

7. Now that Mark has a computer, his typewriter is _____.

8. Many people think computer viruses are quite _____, because they have not experienced one.

Suffix

Study each rule. Then add *–er* to the verb in parentheses and write it on the line.

Add the suffix *–er* to a verb to make a noun. The noun may refer to a person who does the action, or a thing that is used for the action.

Rule 1: If a word ends with a silent *–e*, drop the *–e* and add *–er*.
Example: compute + er = computer

1. (write)   That _____ uses a word processor.

2. (use)   The new computers are _____-friendly.

3. (erase)   Use your "undo" icon like an _____.

4. (trade)   He got it from a _____ on the Internet.

Rule 2: If a word ends in a consonant and *–y*, change the *–y* to *–i* and add *–er*.
Example: copy + er = copier

5. (carry)   He got a _____ for his laptop.

6. (worry)   Don't be such a _____; you won't break the computer!

Rule 3: If a one-syllable word ends in one vowel and one consonant, double the consonant before adding *–er*.
Example: scan + er = scanner

7. (plan)   Use the calendar feature as your _____.

8. (ship)   If you buy something online, use a fast _____.

9. (scan)   Use the _____ to copy the document.

10. (shop)   Not every _____ enjoys Internet auctions.

Rule 4: With all other words, just add *–er*.
Example: print + er = printer

11. (send)   Only open e-mail if you know the _____.

12. (call)   The representative helped the _____.

13. (surf)   A Web _____ can spend many hours on the Internet.

14. (print)   I bought a color _____.

Synonyms

Look at each underlined word or phrase. Choose a word or phrase from the box with a similar meaning and write it on the line.

icon	log off	Save	software
delete	monitor	shut down	surf

1. I love to _____ the Internet. I learn a lot when I <u>browse</u>.

2. You need to _____. If you don't <u>sign off</u>, someone else can use your account.

3. _____ your files on the disk. You can <u>store</u> them there until you need them.

4. Don't <u>turn off</u> the computer until you exit. Then you can _____ the computer.

5. I bought new _____ and I don't understand how the <u>program</u> works.

6. The <u>symbol</u> that looks like an envelope is the _____ for your e-mail.

7. If you _____ that now, you will <u>erase</u> it permanently.

8. He stared at the computer _____, but he couldn't read the words on the <u>screen</u>.

Collocations

Talking about computers involves many two-word collocations.

Choose a word from the box to complete each collocation below.

browser	drive	items	search
button	e-mail	mouse	Web

1. I got a free _____ pad when I bought my computer.

2. My hard _____ crashed.

3. Use the back _____ on your browser.

4. I have a free _____ account.

5. Look in your recycle bin for deleted _____.

6. I want to have my own _____ page.

7. You need a good Web_____ to surf the Internet.

8. Use a _____ engine to find information on the Internet.

Confusing words

In each of the following, circle the word
that best completes the sentence.

Teach and *learn* are both actions that happen in school.
You can *teach* a subject to a person, or you can just say
that you *teach* the person. You can *learn* a subject.

1. Someone (taught/learned) Mark how to use his computer.

2. Mark needed to (teach/learn) about the program before he could use it.

3. Where can I go to (teach/learn) about spreadsheets? I need a good teacher.

4. He (teaches/learns) computer science to high school students.

5. You don't need me to (teach/learn) you how to use a mouse.

6. I think I need to (teach/learn) more about my CPU.

In each of the following, write a form of
say or *tell* on the line.

Say and *tell* are both about talking. Use *say* when you
are talking about the words someone spoke. You can
use *that* after *say*. Use *tell* when you mention both the
speaker and the listener. Use the name of the listener or
a pronoun after *tell*.

7. Mark _____ that he learned a lot in computer class.

8. Mark _____ me that he got a new computer.

9. The sales associate _____ Mark which hardware to buy.

10. Can you _____ me how much a computer costs?

11. He _____ that his mouse wasn't working.

12. He _____ he loves surfing the Internet.

13. We need to _____ him about computer viruses.

14. Mark _____, "Come see my new computer!"

Context Clues

In each of the following, decide if the underlined words have close to the same meaning, or close to the opposite meaning. Write *same* or *opposite* on the line.

> Sentences often contain synonyms or antonyms. We can tell if two words are synonyms or antonyms by the context of the sentence.

_____ 1. You need a password when you <u>log on</u>, but when you <u>log off</u>, you don't.

_____ 2. People use spreadsheets for <u>bookkeeping</u> and <u>accounting</u>.

_____ 3. Mark plans to use his computer for his school <u>work</u>, but he also hopes to <u>play</u> some good games.

_____ 4. He saved a <u>file</u> to his hard drive, and when he went back to work on it later, the <u>document</u> wasn't there.

_____ 5. To some people, a DVD drive is <u>essential</u>. Since I only use my computer for word processing, a DVD drive is a <u>useless</u> piece of hardware for me.

_____ 6. When Mark first shopped for a computer, everything he saw was too <u>expensive</u>. But this time when he went out, he found an <u>affordable</u> model.

_____ 7. Even though the sales associate told me that the instructions on my new game were very <u>clear</u>, when I got it home I found them to be too <u>complicated</u> to understand.

_____ 8. If your e-mail in-box is too full, you should <u>delete</u> some items. But be careful not to <u>erase</u> something you will need later.

_____ 9. Last week an <u>unexpected</u> power outage caused my computer to shut down. When the power company later announced that they <u>planned</u> to turn the power off to fix the lines, I was able to turn my computer off in time.

_____ 10. People recognize that spam or junk e-mail is very <u>common</u>, but they often believe that getting a virus over e-mail is quite <u>rare</u>.

_____ 11. The back of my computer is a jumble of <u>cords</u> and <u>wires</u>.

Parts of Speech

Identify the underlined words. Write *V* on the line if the word is a verb, and write *G* if it is a gerund.

> When we add –*ing* to the base form of a verb, that new word can work like a verb in a continuous tense or like a gerund, which means that it works like a noun. Look for a verb after *be*. Look for a gerund as the subject of the sentence or after a preposition.

_____ 1. She is <u>typing</u> her homework now.

_____ 2. I am careful about <u>saving</u> my documents regularly.

_____ 3. I'm <u>copying</u> the pages right now.

_____ 4. <u>Typing</u> is easy with a word processor.

_____ 5. I'm always worried about <u>deleting</u> important e-mails.

_____ 6. <u>Copying</u> files from one drive to another is easy.

_____ 7. She's <u>saving</u> the files on a CD.

_____ 8. I found the message when I was <u>deleting</u> some old e-mails.

_____ 9. I was <u>typing</u> when the computer crashed.

_____ 10. <u>Deleting</u> old files will make your computer run faster.

Dictionary

Identify the part of speech of each underlined word. Write *N* or *V* on the line. Then look up the word in your dictionary. Choose and write the best definition.

_____ 1. He had to put a new <u>drive</u> in his computer.

definition: _____

_____ 2. I want to get a new <u>mouse</u>.

definition: _____

_____ 3. If we <u>scan</u> the documents, we can save them on a disk.

definition: _____

_____ 4. The programs start when you <u>boot</u> the computer.

definition: _____

_____ 5. You can customize the <u>icons</u> on your computer screen.

definition: _____

Crossword Puzzle

Fill in the puzzle with words from the box.

browser	documents	ISP	ROM	teach	WWW
copier	eraser	memory	save	unplug	
CPU	hardware	monitor	scanner	user	
delete	icon	mouse	software	Web	

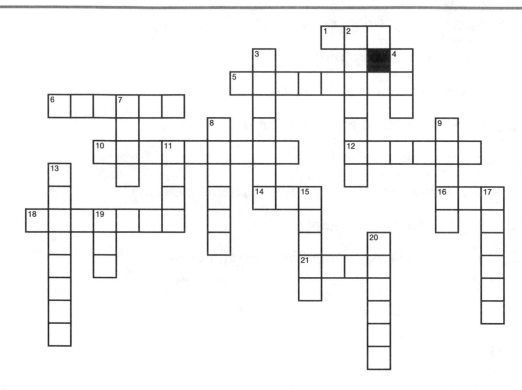

ACROSS

1. _____ stands for *Internet service provider*.
5. My old computer can't run the new _____.
6. My printer is also a _____.
10. You can save all of your _____ on this disk.
12. The delete key is like an _____.
14. I got a new CD-_____ for my computer.
16. You can put the _____ on the floor or on your desk.
18. That site requires a new version of the Web _____.
21. Be sure to _____ before you exit.

DOWN

2. My _____ is also a fax machine.
3. I want a bigger _____.
4. Which _____ site did you look at?
7. Click the _____ that looks like an envelope.
8. My old computer didn't have enough _____.
9. Can you _____ me how to use a spreadsheet?
11. Each _____ has a different password.
13. You need the right _____ and software for the job.
15. Double click the _____ button.
17. You should _____ your computer during a storm.
19. _____ stands for *World Wide Web*.
20. You can _____ files you don't need.

Vocabulary in Context

Choose a word from the box and write it on the line.

CPU	hardware	monitor	printer	scanner

When we moved into our new offices, my manager ordered a lot of new equipment. First, we

got state-of-the-art computer _____. We each got a new

1

_____, a new keyboard, and a high-resolution _____. Then

2   3

each office got a laser _____ and a combination _____/fax

4   5

machine. Setting everything up is our next job!

compact	computer	http	hypertext	memory

When Mark took the Introduction to Personal Computing class, the only test he had was on

initializations. Mark already knew that *PC* stands for personal _____. He had

6

seen _____ and *HTML* in Web addresses, but he didn't know that they stood

7

for _____ transfer protocol and hypertext markup language. Those are difficult

8

words, so Mark was glad that he can just use the initials. Also, Mark knew that *CD* stands for

_____ disk, but when he talked about a CD-ROM, he never knew that *ROM*

9

means read only _____. After Mark studied, he did well on the test.

10

log	off	shut	start

Using a computer is easy. After you _____ up the computer, you have to

11

_____ on with your password. When you are finished with your work,

12

you can either log _____ and leave the computer on, or you can

13

_____ the computer down.

14

Transportation

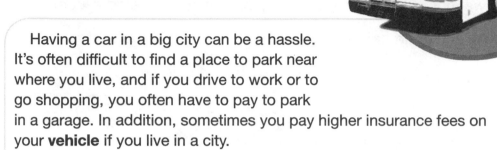

In this lesson, you will work with words about transportation. Read this description of transportation options in a large city.

Having a car in a big city can be a hassle. It's often difficult to find a place to park near where you live, and if you drive to work or to go shopping, you often have to pay to park in a garage. In addition, sometimes you pay higher insurance fees on your **vehicle** if you live in a city.

Nowadays, it is possible to live in a large city without a car. Just look around. You will see a variety of ways to get around that don't require driving yourself. First, there are buses. There seems to be a bus stop on every corner. Dozens of **routes** take you all over the city. Some buses **run** all night, too. Some cities have **subway** systems. The routes are more limited than bus routes. But **subways** can be a convenient way to **commute** to work.

If you don't like mass transportation—buses and subways—you can always walk or ride a bike. If you live in a city, you can get to many places on foot. All of the streets have **sidewalks**. The intersections have **pedestrian** signals. Perhaps you want something quicker than walking. Then you can ride a bike. Some streets even have special bicycle **lanes**.

Traveling from one city to another is not a problem. Many large cities are connected by **rail**, and train stations are conveniently located. You can make reservations on the Internet and show up at the train station about 45 minutes before the train is scheduled to **depart**. If you need to get someplace fast, you can fly. A big city is sure to have an airport. In most cities, a bus or even the subway will drop you at the door of the **terminal**.

All of these convenient **modes** of transportation make it is possible to get along fine without a car.

Definitions

Write each word next to its definition.

commute	mode	route	subway
depart	pedestrian	run	terminal
lane	rails	sidewalk	vehicle

_____ 1. a way from one place to another that is traveled regularly

_____ 2. a large building where people wait to get onto airplanes or buses

_____ 3. to regularly travel back and forth to work

_____ 4. to take people from one place to another on a regular basis; to operate

_____ 5. to leave, especially when starting a trip

_____ 6. part of a road that is marked by painted lines to keep traffic separated

_____ 7. a raised hard surface for walking along the side of a street, usually made of concrete

_____ 8. a form, variety, or manner

_____ 9. a person who is walking, especially on a city street

_____ 10. a machine used for transporting people or things

_____ 11. long steel bars along which trains move

_____ 12. a railroad that runs under the ground

Exercise 2

Airport Codes

Match each airport code below with the city that it represents. Search on the Internet if you can't figure these out.

> Airports are identified by sets of three letters. You can explain these codes with sentences using *stands for*.

_____ 1. ORD

_____ 2. LAX

_____ 3. MIA

_____ 4. JFK

_____ 5. IAD

_____ 6. SFO

_____ 7. MCO

_____ 8. BOS

_____ 9. IAH

a. Washington Dulles International Airport

b. O'Hare International Airport

c. Orlando International Airport

d. Miami International Airport

e. Boston Logan International Airport

f. San Francisco International Airport

g. Los Angeles International Airport

h. George Bush Intercontinental Airport

i. John F. Kennedy International Airport

Exercise 3: Word Builder

Prefixes

Choose a word from the box, add *il*– or *ir*– to it, and write it on the line.

> The prefixes *il*– and *ir*– mean *not* when they are added to adjectives. Use *il*– with words beginning with *l*, and use *ir*– with words beginning with *r*.

legal	literate	resistible
legible	regular	responsible

1. If the bus driver is _____, how does he read the signs?

2. The bus doesn't come at specific times. The schedule is _____.

3. She bought the new sports car. It was _____. She couldn't resist it.

4. It is _____ to drive without a license.

5. The bus driver is responsible for many lives, so it is very _____ of him to drive carelessly.

6. The taxi driver's signature was _____ on the receipt.

Suffixes

Study each rule. Then add *–ful* to the word in parentheses and write it on the line.

> Add the suffix *–ful* to a noun or verb to make an adjective that means *having the characteristic of.*

Rule 1: If a word ends in a consonant and *–y,* change the *–y* to *–i* and add *–ful.*
Example: beauty + ful = beautiful

1. (plenty)   Cabs are usually _____ in New York City.

2. (pity)   The pedestrians looked _____ in the rainstorm.

3. (beauty)   The new trains are _____.

4. (fancy)   The artist proposed a _____ idea for decorating the buses.

Rule 2: Add *–ful* to all other words.
Example: pain + ful = painful

5. (care)   He is a _____ bus driver.

6. (use)   A transportation pass can be very _____.

7. (thought)   The _____ man helped the woman onto the train.

8. (pain)   The twisted ankle was _____, so she didn't walk to work.

9. (forget)   The taxi driver was very _____.

10. (peace)   The city would be _____ if there were no cars or trucks.

11. (color)   The new subway trains are very _____.

12. (harm)   Air pollution can be _____ to your health.

Add *–less* to the word in parentheses and write it on the line.

> Add the suffix *–less* to a noun or verb to make an adjective that means *without the characteristic of.*

13. (care)   _____ drivers cause accidents.

14. (use)   A transportation system is _____ if no one rides it.

15. (thought)   A _____ person left trash on the bus.

16. (color)   Some dangerous gases are _____ and odorless.

Synonyms

Look at each underlined word. Choose a word or phrase from the box with a similar meaning and write it on the line.

> | boats | crossroads | railroads | terminal |
> | car | on foot | streets | travels |

1. In the middle of the night the _____ are empty. There is no one on the <u>roads</u>.

2. You can see _____ in the harbor. Some of the <u>ships</u> are from around the world.

3. I got the ticket at the bus _____. You have to get your ticket at the <u>station</u>.

4. He _____ to his job downtown by bus every day. He hates the <u>commute</u>.

5. There is a stop sign at the _____, so you need to stop at that <u>intersection</u>.

6. I take the <u>train</u> as often as I can because I love _____.

7. I hope I can get there _____, because I love to <u>walk</u>.

8. I stopped my _____ because the sign said that all <u>vehicles</u> must stop.

Collocations

We use some two-word collocations to tell where vehicles stop. Choose a word from the box and write it on the line.

> | bus | stand | terminal |
> | dock | station | train |

1. We waited at the _____ stop on the corner.

2. There were no cabs at the taxi _____.

3. I'll meet you outside the airport _____.

4. We bought our ticket in the _____ station.

5. You have to go underground to get to the subway _____.

6. We got into the canoe at the boat _____.

Confusing Words

In each of the following, circle the word that best completes the sentence.

> *Fee* and *fare* both tell about an amount of money to be paid. A *fee* is an amount of money that you pay to do something. You often pay a fee to professionals for their work. A *fare* is money that you pay to travel on some form of public transportation.

1. The taxi driver had to pay a (fee/fare) to get his license renewed.

2. Let's buy the airline ticket now before the (fees/fares) go up.

3. When I got on the bus, I asked, "How much is the (fee/fare)?"

4. A toll is a kind of (fee/fare) that you pay when you drive on a highway.

5. If you take the train, the (fee/fare) will be a lot less than if you go by plane.

6. You have to consider parking (fees/fares) when you calculate the cost of driving.

In each of the following, write *floor* or *ground* on the line.

> *Floor* and *ground* both tell about what we stand on. A *floor* is inside a building or vehicle, while the *ground* is outdoors.

7. The train was so crowded that some passengers sat on the _____.

8. We sat on the _____ next to the bus stop while we waited for the bus to arrive.

9. The baggage handler left my suitcase on the _____ near where the airplane was parked.

10. The _____ of the bus was very dirty.

11. He thinks he dropped his wallet on the _____ of the taxi.

12. I found five dollars lying on the _____ outside the train station.

13. She left her umbrella on the _____ of the subway station, next to the bench where she was sitting.

14. I think I dropped the change on the _____ after I got out of the taxi.

Context Clues

Copy the two words or phrases with opposite meanings in each of the following.

> When you guess from context, you can often find a word with an opposite meaning in the same sentence to help you. Look for words like *different, but,* or *while* to show that a sentence contains words with opposite meanings.

1. Nothing is ever on schedule. The buses arrive late, while the subway is always early.

   _____   _____

2. While taking the bus is always quite affordable, air travel is usually very expensive.

   _____   _____

3. Speeds on highways are often excessive, while in town they are more moderate.

   _____   _____

4. Although they are both forms of public transportation, an enormous jet can carry hundreds of passengers, while a tiny taxicab can carry just a few.

   _____   _____

5. My flight departed from one gate, but when I returned a few days later, it arrived at a different gate.

   _____   _____

6. At night, the deserted bus station looked different. I was used to seeing it mobbed with people.

   _____   _____

7. At first we thought we were going on the grand cruise ship in the harbor, but then we noticed the simple boat next to it.

   _____   _____

8. A taxi is a costly choice, while a bus is more economical.

   _____   _____

9. If you want to get there fast, take a plane. But if you want a different, more leisurely trip, take a bus or train.

   _____   _____

10. The hardest way to travel in the summer is on foot, while the easiest way is in an air-conditioned taxi.

    _____   _____

Parts of Speech

Identify the underlined words. Write *N* on
the line if the word is a noun, and write *V* if it is a verb.

> Many common vocabulary words can work either as
> nouns or as verbs. Look for a noun after an adjective.
> Look for a verb after a subject or after *to*.

_____ 1. I am going to <u>ship</u> these boxes to New York.

_____ 2. Are you going to <u>ride</u> the bus to school?

_____ 3. We took a nice <u>walk</u> in the park.

_____ 4. I think he has a long <u>commute</u> from his home to his office.

_____ 5. He arrived from Europe on a large <u>ship</u>.

_____ 6. They <u>commute</u> from the suburbs to the city.

_____ 7. Some commuters <u>walk</u> to work.

_____ 8. They had a bumpy <u>ride</u> in the old bus.

Dictionary

Identify the part of speech of each underlined word. Write *N* or *V* on
the line. Then look up the word in your dictionary. Choose and write
the best definition.

_____ 1. The company rented a van to <u>ferry</u> the employees from one office to the other.

definition: _____

_____ 2. The bus stopped about a <u>foot</u> away from the curb.

definition: _____

_____ 3. Who <u>trains</u> the bus drivers?

definition: _____

_____ 4. They are going to <u>truck</u> the products to another state.

definition: _____

_____ 5. The beach is just a short <u>drive</u> from my apartment.

definition: _____

_____ 6. Having a car in the city can be a <u>hassle</u>.

definition: _____

Crossword Puzzle

Fill in the puzzle with words from the box.

boat	fee	LAX	route	stop
careful	floor	pedestrians	sidewalks	streets
commutes	ground	plentiful	stand	terminal
fare	illegible	railroad	station	vehicle

ACROSS

1. I had to wait for 20 minutes at the bus _____.
3. What is the bus _____ in your city?
7. What is the _____ for a taxi license?
8. The license was _____; I couldn't read it.
9. He _____ to work every day by bus.
12. I got a cab outside the train _____.
13. I sat on the _____ next to the bus stop.
15. They got on the _____ at the dock.
16. I hate flying so I travel by _____.
17. The airport code for Los Angeles International airport is _____.
18. Sidewalks are for _____.

DOWN

2. Taxis are _____ in New York City.
4. I got a taxi outside the airport _____.
5. You have to register your _____.
6. There were no taxis at the taxi _____.
9. Be _____ crossing the street.
10. There are bike lanes on some _____.
11. The bus follows the same _____ every day.
12. Bicycles aren't allowed on _____.
14. Some passengers sat on the _____ of the airport terminal.

Vocabulary in Context

Choose a word from the box and write it on the line.

lane	mode	subway	taxis	trucks	vehicles

If you stand on a street in New York, you can see just about every _____ of
                                                                              1
transportation. From the sidewalk, you can see a _____ entrance that takes
                                                                    2
you underground. Then, there is a bicycle _____ next to the sidewalk. In the
                                                          3
right lane of the street, you can see a lot of buses and delivery _____. The
                                                                                4
other lanes are filled with a variety of _____, including _____,
                                                      5   6
cars, and motorcycles.

beautiful	careful	colorful	peaceful	plentiful

We wish to welcome tourists to our _____ city! We hope you have a great
                                                    7
time on your visit. You don't need your car, since taxis are _____. Ask the
                                                                           8
driver to show you the _____ murals on the sides of many buildings. There is
                                    9
a lot of traffic on our streets, so please be _____ when you cross. If you want
                                                            10
a _____ moment away from the traffic, please visit our park.
          11

fare	fee	floor	ground	stop

Ed wanted to visit the art museum. He put the money for the bus _____ in
                                                                               12
one pocket, and the money for the entrance _____ in the other pocket. At the
                                                          13
bus _____, he took money out of the wrong pocket. When he was putting it
          14
back, he thinks he dropped a dollar on the _____ of the bus. When he got to
                                                          15
the museum, he didn't have enough money to enter. He sat down on the

_____ and thought about what to do.
          16

Advertising

In this lesson, you will work with words about advertising. Read this story about how advertisements convinced Sarah to buy a product.

Last week, Sarah's friends told her about a new kitchen **gadget**. It can chop fruits and vegetables. It also makes juices. The gadget is called ChopJuice/4000. Her friends had just bought one. Sarah thought that the conversation was **informative**. But she was not interested in buying the gadget.

The next day, Sarah was listening to the radio. She heard a public service **announcement** from her city's health department. The announcer **urged** people to eat more fruits and vegetables. Sarah thought about the ChopJuice/4000. But she thought she might be able to eat more fruits and vegetables without actually buying a fancy gadget.

Later, Sarah turned on the TV. A **commercial** came on. What was the commercial for? It was for the ChopJuice/4000! The commercial demonstrated how easy the gadget is to use. Sarah still wasn't **convinced**. Then she started looking for something else to watch. She noticed an **infomercial** on a cable channel. It was a half-hour show about the ChopJuice/4000. Two people were demonstrating how to make salads and juices. The audience **applauded** every few minutes. Sarah knew that the whole show was a big advertisement. She knew the people were paid to applaud. But she was starting to think that she just might need to buy this **useful** gadget.

Sarah turned off the television and got into her car. She had an appointment with her doctor for a checkup. While she was driving, she saw a **billboard**. You guessed it. The billboard was advertising the ChopJuice/4000. The **slogan** on the billboard said, "Eat Right." When Sarah got to her doctor's office, she sat in the waiting room. She opened a magazine. The first **advertisement** that she saw was for the ChopJuice/4000. Sarah didn't stay for her appointment. She left the doctor's office and drove straight to the mall.

Definitions

Write each word next to its definition.

advertisement	billboard	gadget	slogan
announcement	commercial	infomercial	urge
applaud	convinced	informative	useful

_____ 1. a phrase used in advertising

_____ 2. a long commercial in the form of a television program

_____ 3. a public notice that tells people about things to buy

_____ 4. having a practical purpose

_____ 5. a message that is broadcast to the public

_____ 6. feeling sure about something

_____ 7. to suggest strongly or try to persuade

_____ 8. to express approval by clapping hands

_____ 9. a large sign used for advertising that is usually found next to a highway

_____ 10. providing useful facts and ideas

_____ 11. a small machine or tool that is used for a particular task

_____ 12. a paid advertisement on TV or radio

Portmanteaus

Match the portmanteaus below with the words that were combined to create them.

> Portmanteaus (pronounced /port-man-toze/) are blended words. You can explain a portmanteau with sentences using *is a combination of.*

_____ 1. brunch   a. motor and pedal

_____ 2. camcorder   b. smoke and fog

_____ 3. infomercial   c. sports and broadcast

_____ 4. spork   d. breakfast and lunch

_____ 5. motel   e. camera and recorder

_____ 6. Spanglish   f. motor and hotel

_____ 7. moped   g. Spanish and English

_____ 8. sportscast   h. information and commercial

_____ 9. smog   i. spoon and fork

Exercise 3: **Word Builder**

Prefixes

Choose a word from the box, add *in–* or *im–* to it, and write it on the line.

> The prefixes *in–* and *im–* can mean *not* when they are added to adjectives. Use *in–* with words beginning with some consonants, including *c, d,* and *s,* or with a vowel, and use *im–* with words beginning with *m* or *p.*

> **accurate**   **direct**   **patient**   **sufficient**
> **capable**   **mature**   **possible**

1. It is _____ to get the results they show on TV. You just can't do it.

2. Some people are _____ of resisting advertisements. They just can't resist.

3. Just telling someone about a product is _____. It's not enough.

4. Children, who are _____, often believe most commercials.

5. Some commercials make _____ claims when they give the wrong information.

6. I get _____ when there are too many commercials on TV.

7. Placing products in movies is a kind of _____ advertising.

Suffix

Study each rule. Then add *–ive* to the
word in parentheses and write it on the line.

> Add the suffix *–ive* to a verb to make an adjective that
> shows that an action is probable.

Rule 1: If a word ends in a silent *–e*, drop the *–e* and add *–ive*.
Example: create + ive = creative

1. (cooperate)   Her friend was very _____.

2. (negate)   I don't like _____ ads.

3. (create)   The ad was very _____.

4. (emote)   He is an _____ person.

**Rule 2: If a word ends in *–d* or *–de*, drop the final letter(s) and
       add *–sive*.**
Example: extend + ive = extensive

5. (expend)   That gadget is too _____.

6. (conclude)   They had _____ evidence.

7. (persuade)   His argument is _____.

8. (offend)   I don't like _____ ads.

9. (explode)   That chemical is _____.

10. (extend)   They did _____ research.

Rule 3: If a word ends in *–ss* or *–ct*, add *–ive*.
Example: act + ive = active

11. (attract)   They use _____ people in the ads.

12. (pass)   It is a form of _____ advertising.

13. (select)   They are very _____.

14. (progress)   It is a _____ verb form.

15. (interact)   That exhibit is _____.

Synonyms

Look at each underlined word. Choose a word from the box with a similar meaning and write it on the line.

| announcement | conversation | notify | persuade |
| billboards | devices | pamphlets | |

1. I heard an important _____ on the radio. It was a <u>message</u> about a bad storm.

2. I hardly ever have a whole _____ with my neighbor, but yesterday we had a nice <u>chat</u>.

3. I love reading the _____ on the highway. In some places there are more than 10 <u>signs</u> per mile.

4. Some people are easy to _____, but you can't <u>convince</u> me easily.

5. Some advertisers produce <u>brochures</u> or _____ describing their products.

6. The company will _____ you if there is a problem. They can <u>inform</u> you by mail.

7. My kitchen is full of fancy <u>gadgets</u>, but I only use about half of the _____.

Collocations

Choose a word from the box and write it on the line.

> English uses some two–, three–, and four-word collocations to talk about advertising.

| channels | commercial | magazine | service |
| classified | free | popup | |

1. The announcer said the program would be back after the _____ break.

2. They used color pictures of the product in the _____ ad.

3. When I am on the Internet, I don't like all of the _____ ads.

4. If you want to sell something yourself, you can buy a _____ ad.

5. The TV station has to play public _____ announcements daily.

6. One way to advertise is to give away _____ samples.

7. If you want to see an infomercial, flip through your cable _____ late at night.

Confusing Words

In each of the following, circle the word that best completes the sentence.

Hope and *wish* both tell about wanting something. *Hope* tells about wanting something that is possible. *Wish* tells about wanting something that is probably not possible. Use present modals *(can, will)* after *hope* to show possibility; use past modals *(could, would)* after *wish* to show that something is unlikely or impossible.

1. I (hope/wish) I can buy a new TV soon.

2. I (hope/wish) I could watch a TV show without commercials.

3. Sarah (hopes/wishes) she could afford everything she sees on TV.

4. She (hopes/wishes) she will save enough for the new car by next year.

5. Don't you (hope/wish) that ads would just disappear from the TV?

6. I (hope/wish) those ads would stop popping up when I surf the Internet.

7. Dan (hopes/wishes) he will be working in advertising next year.

8. Ann (hopes/wishes) she can rent that movie and watch it without commercials.

In each of the following, write *very* or *too* on the line.

Very and *too* are intensifiers. *Very* tells that an adjective is stronger than normal. *Too* is used before an adjective to tell about some negative result. For example, if we say, "That is very expensive," *very* intensifies the word *expensive*. However, if we say, "That is too expensive," we imply that we cannot buy it.

9. That gadget is _____ big. It won't fit in my kitchen.

10. The TV commercial is _____ funny. Everyone laughs at it.

11. I am _____ interested in that product. I think I'll buy it.

12. There are _____ many ads in that magazine, so I don't buy it.

13. I had to turn off my TV because the commercials were _____ loud.

14. The public service announcement was _____ informative.

Context Clues

In each of the following, decide if the
underlined words have close to the same meaning or close to the opposite
meaning. Write *same* or *opposite* on the line.

Sentences often contain synonyms or antonyms. We
can tell if two words are synonyms or antonyms by the
context of the sentence.

_____ 1. Most ads try to <u>persuade</u> you to buy one product and <u>discourage</u> you from buying the competitor's product.

_____ 2. Most people hate infomercials, but I love them. I find them <u>informative</u> and <u>educational</u>.

_____ 3. During the infomercial, there is always some kind of <u>discussion</u> that sounds like an informal <u>conversation</u>.

_____ 4. TV stations don't <u>accept</u> every ad that companies want to broadcast. In fact, they <u>reject</u> about half of them.

_____ 5. You can use classified ads to <u>buy</u> something you need and to <u>sell</u> something that you don't need.

_____ 6. A lot of TV ads are accompanied by <u>jingles</u>. The advertisers think <u>songs</u> will help people remember their product.

_____ 7. First we will have some <u>announcements</u>, and after those <u>messages</u> the meeting will start.

_____ 8. I wanted to ride my <u>moped</u> to school, but then I saw a sign that said <u>scooters</u> are not allowed on school grounds.

_____ 9. Even though I am <u>incapable</u> of learning some things, I am <u>able</u> to do well in school.

_____ 10. I think political advertisements should always be <u>positive</u>. <u>Negative</u> advertisements aren't good for anyone.

_____ 11. The TV station broadcast an <u>inaccurate</u> public service announcement yesterday. Today they apologized and broadcast the <u>correct</u> information.

_____ 12. The <u>smog</u> is just terrible. <u>Air pollution</u> is a real problem in that city.

Parts of Speech

Identify the underlined words. Write *V*
on the line if the word is a verb, and
write *G* if it is a gerund.

> When we add *–ing* to the base form of a verb, that new
> word can work like a verb in a continuous tense or like a
> gerund, which behaves like a noun. Look for a verb after
> *be.* Look for a gerund as the subject of the sentence or
> after a preposition.

_____ 1. Some advertisers try to sell new products by <u>demonstrating</u> them in stores.

_____ 2. The company is thinking about <u>introducing</u> a new product.

_____ 3. That company is <u>advertising</u> their new products.

_____ 4. Advertisers are <u>persuading</u> us to try new items.

_____ 5. <u>Advertising</u> on television is expensive.

_____ 6. The announcer is <u>introducing</u> the commercial now.

_____ 7. He's <u>demonstrating</u> how the new vacuum works.

_____ 8. <u>Persuading</u> children to try new cookies is not difficult.

_____ 9. Most infomercials are for <u>introducing</u> new products.

Dictionary

Identify the part of speech of each underlined word. Write *N* or *V* on
the line. Then look up the word in your dictionary. Choose and write
the best definition.

_____ 1. I saw a <u>sign</u> introducing a new burger at the fast food restaurant.

definition: _____

_____ 2. Since TV commercials are so expensive, we could only afford a 30-second <u>spot</u>.

definition: _____

_____ 3. Cartoons usually have commercials that <u>urge</u> children to try new cereals.

definition: _____

_____ 4. Last night's news <u>broadcast</u> was interrupted by 15 commercials.

definition: _____

_____ 5. Some people think that TV <u>subjects</u> children to too many commercials.

definition: _____

Crossword Puzzle

Fill in the puzzle with words from the box.

advertisement	billboards	creative	informative	persuasive	service
applaud	break	expensive	jingle	popup	sponsor
attractive	cable	gadget	pamphlet	sample	spot

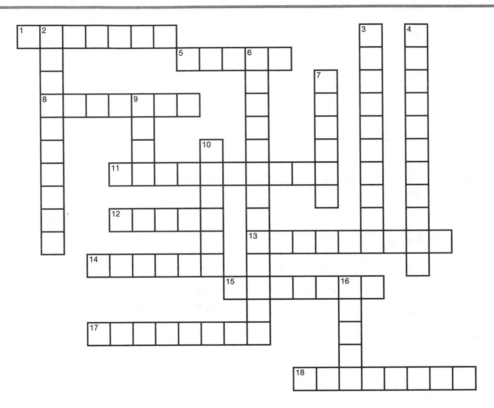

ACROSS

1. The audience gets paid to _____.
5. The program will return after a commercial _____.
8. They always stop for "a word from our _____."
11. Models are usually _____.
12. I have a lot of _____ ads on my computer.
13. Superbowl commercials are _____.
14. He was singing the _____ from the commercial.
15. The station had to broadcast a public _____ announcement.
17. The _____ had a lot of information about the product.
18. The writers have to be _____.

DOWN

2. The infomercial host was _____.
3. We passed dozens of _____ on the highway.
4. Many people think ads are _____ because they can learn from them.
6. I saw an _____ in a magazine for that.
7. My friend buys a new _____ every week.
9. They could only afford a 30-second _____.
10. I got a free _____ in the mail.
16. I watch infomercials on the _____ channel.

Vocabulary in Context

Choose a word from the box and write it on the line.

advertisements	billboards	commercials	Slogans

Some children see too many _____ nowadays. If they watch TV, they see
_____ 1

several _____ every hour. When they learn how to read, they see
_____ 2

_____ and signs everywhere. _____ are some of the first
_____ 3 _____ 4

words that many children learn.

brunch	moped	motel	smog	Spanglish	spork

Sarah took a trip to Los Angeles. The day before she left, she learned a new word:

portmanteau. Sarah was surprised at how many portmanteaus she used on her trip. First, she

ate _____ on the plane. She ate her fruit salad with a _____.
_____ 5 _____ 6

As soon as they approached Los Angeles, Sarah noticed the _____. After she
_____ 7

landed, Sarah went to her _____. When she went to the front desk to ask
_____ 8

about renting a _____ to tour the area, Sarah noticed that the clerks were
_____ 9

speaking _____. Sarah smiled at how many portmanteaus she was using.
_____ 10

attractive	informative	negative	offensive	persuasive

People who make TV commercials have a hard job. Commercials have to be

_____, so people will learn something, and _____ so people
_____ 11 _____ 12

will buy the product. They can't be _____ or _____. And if
_____ 13 _____ 14

they hire actors, the actors must be _____.
_____ 15

Answer Key

Lesson 1

Exercise 1, p. 9

1. kindergarten
2. compulsory
3. diploma
4. academic
5. vocational
6. graduate
7. enroll
8. college
9. elementary school
10. subject
11. public
12. prepare

Exercise 2, p. 10

1. g   2. e   3. f   4. b   5. c   6. h   7. d   8. a

Exercise 3, p. 10

1. re-enroll
2. reread
3. retake
4. recharge
5. rebuilt
6. replay
7. rewrite
8. reset
9. refill

Exercise 4, p. 11

1. graduation
2. cooperation
3. concentration
4. abbreviation
5. subtraction
6. suggestion
7. interruption
8. invention
9. correction
10. reduction
11. production
12. introduction
13. invasion
14. explosion
15. division
16. decision

Exercise 5, p. 12

1. noisy
2. public
3. together
4. optional
5. present
6. formal

Exercise 6, p. 12

1. up
2. off
3. off
4. from
5. by
6. from, to
7. out of
8. out

Exercise 7, p. 13

1. take
2. spent
3. took
4. take
5. takes
6. spend
7. takes
8. spend
9. wasted
10. spends
11. spend
12. wasted
13. waste
14. spend

Exercise 8, p. 14

1. principal; definition
2. community college; definition
3. subjects; examples
4. electives; examples
5. report card; definition
6. arithmetic; examples
7. higher education; examples
8. tutor; definition
9. graduate; definition
10. preschool; definition
11. vocational schools; definition
12. stringed instruments; examples
13. playground equipment; examples
14. recess; definition

Exercise 9, p. 15

1. V   3. N   5. V   7. N   9. V
2. N   4. V   6. N   8. N   10. V

Exercise 10, p. 15

Definitions will vary.
1. N   2. N   3. N   4. N   5. V

Review 1, p. 16

Across

3. tutor
5. college
7. principal
11. diploma
12. reunion
13. GED
14. subject
15. ESL
16. off
17. snack

Down

1. attend
2. drop
4. vocational
6. vary
8. absent
9. playground
10. takes

Review 2, p. 17

1. kindergarten
2. elementary
3. secondary
4. college
5. university
6. reread
7. replay
8. rewrite
9. retake
10. re-enroll
11. schedules
12. subjects
13. graduation
14. electives
15. diploma

Lesson 2

Exercise 1, p. 19

1. witness
2. investigate
3. arrest
4. crime
5. victim
6. kidnap
7. murder
8. punish
9. criminal
10. shoplift
11. vandalism
12. robbery

Exercise 2, p. 20

1. e   2. c   3. h   4. a   5. b   6. d   7. f   8. g

Exercise 3, p. 20

1. disconnect
2. disagree
3. disadvantage
4. disrespectful
5. Dishonest
6. disqualify

Exercise 4, p. 21

1. Stopping
2. Robbing
3. Hitting
4. Running
5. Investigating
6. Fining
7. Moving
8. Chasing
9. Firing
10. Stealing
11. Shoplifting
12. Shooting
13. Witnessing
14. Repairing
15. Finding
16. Staying

Exercise 5, p. 22

1. death   2. lie   3. freed   4. violent   5. safe   6. low

Exercise 6, p. 22

1. assault
2. cheat
3. punishment
4. jury
5. against
6. crime
7. break
8. house

Exercise 7, p. 23

1. robbed
2. robbed
3. stole
4. steal
5. robbed
6. rob
7. robbed
8. stolen
9. Drop
10. fell
11. fell
12. dropped
13. fell
14. dropped
15. fell
16. fell

Exercise 8, p. 24

1. burglars, robbers
2. battery, assault
3. shoplifting, stealing
4. lawyer, attorney
5. killing, murder
6. gun, weapon
7. shoot, fire
8. detective, investigator
9. vandalism, destroying property
10. against the law, illegal

Exercise 9, p. 25

1. N   3. V   5. V   7. N   9. N
2. V   4. N   6. V   8. V   10. N

Exercise 10, p. 25

Definitions will vary.
1. N   2. N   3. V   4. N   5. N

Review 1, p. 26

Across

2. burglar
4. sentenced
9. violations
10. victim
12. HQ
13. kidnap
14. fine
15. jury
17. investigating

Down

1. vandalism
3. arrest
5. criminal
6. witness
7. DOA
8. dishonest
11. murder
16. fired
18. AKA

Review 2, p. 27

1. crime
2. shoplifting
3. vandalism
4. robbery
5. murder
6. disadvantages
7. dishonest
8. disconnected
9. disrespectful
10. disagrees
11. fired
12. gun
13. shot
14. rob
15. steal

Lesson 3

Exercise 1, p. 29

1. serve
2. elect
3. enforce
4. federal
5. propose
6. veto
7. approve
8. branch
9. appoint
10. term
11. balance
12. create

Exercise 2, p. 30

1. c   2. h   3. d   4. i   5. f   6. e   7. b   8. g   9. a

Exercise 3, p. 30

1. interconnected
2. international
3. intercity
4. intercontinental
5. interrelated
6. interdependent
7. interstate
8. interoffice

Exercise 4, p. 31

1. federally
2. nationally
3. locally
4. personally
5. possibly
6. Remarkably
7. responsibly
8. happily
9. easily
10. busily
11. patriotically
12. logically
13. realistically
14. Historically

Exercise 5, p. 32

1. agency
2. appointed
3. recommendation
4. justice
5. reject
6. national

Exercise 6, p. 32

1. holding
2. take
3. takes
4. holds
5. hold
6. took

Exercise 7, p. 33

1. capitol
2. capital
3. capitol
4. capital
5. capitol
6. capital
7. capital
8. principal
9. principal
10. principles
11. principal
12. principle

Exercise 8, p. 34

1. elected, appointed
2. rejected, accepted
3. local, federal
4. regulated, free
5. tired, resigned
6. boring, interesting
7. agrees, opposed
8. pleased, disappointed
9. calm, troubled
10. aware, ignorant

Exercise 9, p. 35

1. V   3. Adj.   5. V   7. V   9. Adj.
2. Adj.   4. V   6. Adj.   8. V   10. V

Exercise 10, p. 35

Definitions will vary.
1. N   2. N   3. V   4. Adj.   5. N

Review 1, p. 36

Across

2. elections
4. vetoes
6. appoints
11. Rep.
12. enforce
15. branches
16. elect
17. capitol
19. justice
20. agency

Down

1. govt.
3. term
5. Sen.
7. principle
8. federal
9. holds
10. serve
13. effect
14. balances
15. takes

Review 2, p. 37

1. justices
2. elected
3. appointed
4. selects
5. approve
6. nomination
7. elections
8. effect
9. officials
10. office
11. Intercity
12. interstate
13. interconnected
14. international

Lesson 4

Exercise 1, p. 39

1. film
2. play
3. orchestra
4. hall
5. band
6. performance
7. club
8. entertainment
9. purchase
10. concert
11. downtown
12. talent

Exercise 2, p. 40

1. g   2. c   3. f   4. b   5. d   6. h   7. e   8. a

Exercise 3, p. 40

1. multimillionaire
2. multilingual
3. multicolored
4. multipurpose
5. multifamily
6. multinational
7. multimedia
8. multicultural

Exercise 4, p. 41

1. entertainment
2. enjoyment
3. agreement
4. movement
5. improvement
6. requirement
7. importance
8. tolerance
9. distance
10. elegance
11. performance
12. Attendance
13. disturbance
14. appearance
15. assistance

Exercise 5, p. 42

1. likes   2. film   3. talents   4. forms   5. amuse   6. buy

Exercise 6, p. 42

1. concert
2. movie
3. baseball
4. amusement
5. game
6. night
7. circus
8. art

Exercise 7, p. 43

1. listened
2. heard
3. hear
4. heard
5. Listen
6. listen
7. hear
8. listen
9. amusing
10. amused
11. amusing
12. amusing
13. amused
14. amusing
15. amused
16. amusing

Exercise 8, p. 44

1. violins, violas
2. concert hall, theater
3. entertainers, performers
4. films, movies
5. play, production
6. museums, galleries
7. piccolo, flute
8. amused, entertained
9. conducts, directs
10. dance, ballet
11. enjoys, likes
12. forms, type

Exercise 9, p. 45

1. N   3. V   5. V   7. V   9. N
2. V   4. V   6. N   8. N   10. V

Exercise 10, p. 45

Definitions will vary.
1. N   2. N   3. N   4. V   5. V

Review 1, p. 46

Across

3. listen
5. talented
7. club
8. Wed.
9. tent
10. hall
11. improvement
12. appearance
15. art
16. orchestra

Down

1. multimedia
2. baseball
4. entertainment
6. amusing
13. plays
14. Aft.

Review 2, p. 47

1. band
2. film
3. concert
4. performance
5. play
6. hall
7. club
8. museum
9. park
10. theater
11. stadium
12. multipurpose
13. Multicultural
14. multilingual
15. multinational

Lesson 5

Exercise 1, p. 49

1. pedal
2. trunk
3. windshield
4. clutch
5. upholstery
6. dashboard
7. transmission
8. fenders
9. hood
10. bumper
11. hubcap
12. ignition

Exercise 2, p. 50

1. c   2. a   3. g   4. d   5. f   6. h   7. e   8. b

Exercise 3, p. 50

1. preteen
2. precaution
3. prearrange
4. prepay
5. preview
6. prefabricated
7. pre-owned
8. pretest

Exercise 4, p. 51

1. relationship
2. ownership
3. membership
4. championship
5. partnership
6. stability
7. ability
8. possibility
9. intensity
10. creativity
11. reality
12. priority
13. popularity

Exercise 5, p. 52

1. parking brake
2. steer
3. brake
4. gas pedal
5. accelerate
6. honk the horn

Exercise 6, p. 52

1. up
2. down
3. up
4. on
5. in, in
6. on
7. up, on
8. on

Exercise 7, p. 53

1. invention
2. invented
3. discovered
4. discovered
5. invented
6. invention
7. discovered
8. invention
9. discovered
10. brake
11. break
12. brake
13. break
14. break
15. brake
16. break
17. brake

Exercise 8, p. 54

1. battery; definition
2. safety equipment; examples
3. speedometer; definition
4. optional equipment; examples
5. brake lights; definition
6. accelerate; definition
7. standard equipment; examples
8. trunk; definition
9. passengers; definition
10. axle; definition
11. traffic violations; examples
12. entertainment; examples
13. odometer; definition
14. sedan; definition

Exercise 9, p. 55

1. adv.
2. adv.
3. adj.
4. adj.
5. adj.
6. adv.
7. adj.
8. adj.
9. adv.
10. adv.

Exercise 10, p. 55

Definitions will vary.
1. N   2. V   3. N   4. V   5. N

Review 1, p. 56

Across

2. ownership
6. trunk
8. bumper
10. GM
11. up
14. accelerate
16. brake
18. down
19. steer

Down

1. Mpg
3. windshield
4. honk
5. hubcaps
7. ignition
9. possibility
12. preview
13. safety
15. on
17. AC

Review 2, p. 57

1. dashboard
2. pedals
3. hood
4. upholstery
5. prearrange
6. preview
7. pretest
8. prepay
9. precautions
10. in
11. in
12. on
13. down
14. up
15. on
16. on
17. on

Lesson 6

Exercise 1, p. 59

1. fracture
2. sprain
3. bacteria
4. pediatrician
5. swell
6. physician
7. clinic
8. prescription
9. anemic
10. veterinarian
11. fever
12. infection

Exercise 2, p. 60

1. e   2. h   3. a   4. c   5. d   6. i   7. b   8. f   9. g

Exercise 3, p. 60

1. overeat
2. overcrowded
3. overworked
4. overestimated
5. overcharged
6. overpriced
7. overcook
8. overflow
9. overruled

Exercise 4, p. 61

1. biologist
2. psychologist
3. zoologist
4. technologist
5. therapist
6. journalist
7. artist
8. receptionist
9. pediatrician
10. optician
11. diagnostician
12. mathematician

Exercise 5, p. 62

1. overweight
2. heat
3. worried
4. elderly
5. energetic
6. discharged
7. awake
8. well

Exercise 6, p. 62

1. technician
2. hygienist
3. specialist
4. administrator
5. therapist
6. aide
7. emergency

Exercise 7, p. 63

1. affect
2. effects
3. affect
4. affects
5. effects
6. effects
7. effects
8. affects
9. advice
10. advice
11. advice
12. advise
13. advise
14. advice
15. advise
16. advise

Exercise 8, p. 64

1. same
2. same
3. opposite
4. opposite
5. same
6. opposite
7. opposite
8. opposite
9. same
10. same
11. same
12. opposite
13. same
14. same
15. same

Exercise 9, p. 65

1. V
2. adj.
3. adj.
4. adj.
5. V
6. V
7. V
8. adj.
9. adj.
10. adj.

Exercise 10, p. 65

Definitions will vary.
1. N   2. V   3. N   4. V   5. N

Review 1, p. 66

Across

1. tablet
4. ER
6. overeat
8. swell
9. overcharge
11. receptionist
13. overweight

Down

2. effects
3. veterinarian
4. energetic
5. anemic
7. therapist
9. optician
10. fever
11. RN
12. well

Review 2, p. 67

1. pediatrician
2. infection
3. fractured
4. sprained
5. advised
6. ER
7. MRI
8. OR
9. IV
10. ICU
11. overworked
12. overcrowded
13. overcharged
14. overcooked
15. overpriced

Lesson 7

Exercise 1, p. 69

1. passbook
2. financial
3. check
4. loan
5. charge
6. debit
7. deposit
8. interest
9. cash
10. savings
11. withdraw
12. credit

Exercise 2, p. 70

1. e   2. h   3. a   4. f   5. d   6. g   7. c   8. b

Exercise 3, p. 70

1. mispronounces
2. misplaced
3. misunderstood
4. misinformed
5. mismanaged
6. misdirected
7. miscounted
8. misspelled
9. miscalculated

Exercise 4, p. 71

1. refusal
2. arrival
3. appraisal
4. survival
5. proposal
6. burial
7. denial
8. trial
9. withdrawal
10. dismissal
11. portrayal
12. betrayal

Exercise 5, p. 72

1. deposited
2. borrow
3. spend
4. high
5. outside
6. fake
7. penalty
8. careful

Exercise 6, p. 72

1. back
2. off
3. visit
4. off
5. to
6. for
7. up
8. attention

Exercise 7, p. 73

1. borrow
2. lent
3. borrow
4. borrow
5. lend
6. lend
7. borrow
8. borrow
9. there
10. There
11. their
12. their
13. there
14. their
15. their
16. there

Exercise 8, p. 74

1. debit; definition
2. invest; definition
3. banking documents; examples
4. savings account; definition
5. cash; examples
6. charges; examples
7. account balance; definition
8. interest; definition
9. transactions; examples
10. appraisal; definition
11. personal identification number; definition
12. home improvement; examples

Exercise 9, p. 75

1. N   2. V   3. N   4. V   5. N   6. N   7. V   8. V

Exercise 10, p. 75

Definitions will vary.
1. V   2. N   3. V   4. N   5. N

Review 1, p. 76

Across

1. deposit
3. ATM
6. back
10. interest
12. misunderstood
13. safe
15. misplaced
16. balance
18. withdraw

Down

2. passbook
3. appraisal
4. There
5. invest
6. borrow
7. cash
8. misdirected
9. SSN
11. their
14. PIN
17. lend

Review 2, p. 77

1. financial
2. checking
3. savings
4. invest
5. CD
6. loans
7. interest
8. mismanaged
9. miscounted
10. mispronounces
11. misspelled
12. misinformed
13. attention
14. to
15. for
16. back
17. off

Lesson 8

Exercise 1, p. 79

1. monitor
2. crash
3. software
4. browser
5. virus
6. spreadsheet
7. drive
8. hardware
9. log on
10. memory
11. scanner
12. document

Exercise 2, p. 80

1. d   2. c   3. e   4. h   5. i   6. g   7. f   8. a   9. b

Exercise 3, p. 80

1. unable
2. unregulated
3. unfamiliar
4. unplugged
5. unreadable
6. unexpected
7. unnecessary
8. uncommon

Exercise 4, p. 81

1. writer
2. user
3. eraser
4. trader
5. carrier
6. worrier
7. planner
8. shipper
9. scanner
10. shopper
11. sender
12. caller
13. surfer
14. printer

Exercise 5, p. 82

1. surf
2. log off
3. Save
4. shut down
5. software
6. icon
7. delete
8. monitor

Exercise 6, p 82

1. mouse
2. drive
3. button
4. e-mail
5. items
6. Web
7. browser
8. search

Exercise 7, p. 83

1. taught
2. learn
3. learn
4. teaches
5. teach
6. learn
7. said
8. told
9. told
10. tell
11. said
12. said
13. tell
14. said

Exercise 8, p. 84

1. opposite
2. same
3. opposite
4. same
5. opposite
6. opposite
7. opposite
8. same
9. opposite
10. opposite
11. same

Exercise 9, p. 85

1. V   3. V   5. G   7. V   9. V
2. G   4. G   6. G   8. V   10. G

Exercise 10, p. 85

Definitions will vary.
1. N   2. N   3. V   4. V   5. N

Review 1, p. 86

Across

1. ISP
5. software
6. copier
10. documents
12. eraser
14. ROM
16. CPU
18. browser
21. save

Down

2. scanner
3. monitor
4. Web
7. icon
8. memory
9. teach
11. user
13. hardware
15. mouse
17. unplug
19. WWW
20. delete

Review 2, p. 87

1. hardware
2. CPU
3. monitor
4. printer
5. scanner
6. computer
7. http
8. hypertext
9. compact
10. memory
11. start
12. log
13. off
14. shut

Lesson 9

Exercise 1, p. 89

1. route
2. terminal
3. commute
4. run
5. depart
6. lane
7. sidewalk
8. mode
9. pedestrian
10. vehicle
11. rails
12. subway

Exercise 2, p. 90

1. b   2. g   3. d   4. i   5. a   6. f   7. c   8. e   9. h

Exercise 3, p. 90

1. illiterate
2. irregular
3. irresistible
4. illegal
5. irresponsible
6. illegible

Exercise 4, p. 91

1. plentiful
2. pitiful
3. beautiful
4. fanciful
5. careful
6. useful
7. thoughtful
8. painful
9. forgetful
10. peaceful
11. colorful
12. harmful
13. Careless
14. useless
15. thoughtless
16. colorless

Exercise 5, p. 92

1. streets
2. boats
3. terminal
4. travels
5. crossroads
6. railroads
7. on foot
8. car

Exercise 6, p. 92

1. bus
2. stand
3. terminal
4. train
5. station
6. dock

Exercise 7, p. 93

1. fee
2. fares
3. fare
4. fee
5. fare
6. fees
7. floor
8. ground
9. ground
10. floor
11. floor
12. ground
13. floor
14. ground

Exercise 8, p. 94

1. late, early
2. affordable, expensive
3. excessive, moderate
4. enormous, tiny
5. departed, returned
6. deserted, mobbed
7. grand, simple
8. costly, economical
9. fast, leisurely
10. hardest, easiest

Exercise 9, p. 95

1. V   2. V   3. N   4. N   5. N   6. V   7. V   8. N

Exercise 10, p. 95

Definitions will vary.
1. V   2. N   3. V   4. V   5. N   6. N

Review 1, p. 96

Across

1. stop
3. fare
7. fee
8. illegible
9. commutes
12. station
13. ground
15. boat
16. railroad
17. LAX
18. pedestrians

Down

2. plentiful
4. terminal
5. vehicle
6. stand
9. careful
10. streets
11. route
12. sidewalks
14. floor

Review 2, p. 97

1. mode
2. subway
3. lane
4. trucks
5. vehicles
6. taxis
7. beautiful
8. plentiful
9. colorful
10. careful
11. peaceful
12. fare
13. fee
14. stop
15. floor
16. ground

Lesson 10

Exercise 1, p. 99

1. slogan
2. infomercial
3. advertisement
4. useful
5. announcement
6. convinced
7. urge
8. applaud
9. billboard
10. informative
11. gadget
12. commercial

Exercise 2, p. 100

1. d   2. e   3. h   4. i   5. f   6. g   7. a   8. c   9. b

Exercise 3, p. 100

1. impossible
2. incapable
3. insufficient
4. immature
5. inaccurate
6. impatient
7. indirect

Exercise 4, p. 101

1. cooperative
2. negative
3. creative
4. emotive
5. expensive
6. conclusive
7. persuasive
8. offensive
9. explosive
10. extensive
11. attractive
12. passive
13. selective
14. progressive
15. interactive

Exercise 5, p. 102

1. announcement
2. conversation
3. billboards
4. persuade
5. pamphlets
6. notify
7. devices

Exercise 6, p. 102

1. commercial
2. magazine
3. popup
4. classified
5. service
6. free
7. channels

Exercise 7, p. 103

1. hope
2. wish
3. wishes
4. hopes
5. wish
6. wish
7. hopes
8. hopes
9. too
10. very
11. very
12. too
13. too
14. very

Exercise 8, p. 104

1. opposite
2. same
3. same
4. opposite
5. opposite
6. same
7. same
8. same
9. opposite
10. opposite
11. opposite
12. same

Exercise 9, p. 105

1. G   2. G   3. V   4. V   5. G   6. V   7. V   8. G   9. G

Exercise 10, p. 105

Definitions will vary.
1. N   2. N   3. V   4. N   5. V

Review 1, p. 106

Across

1. applaud
5. break
8. sponsor
11. attractive
12. popup
13. expensive
14. jingle
15. service
17. pamphlet
18. creative

Down

2. persuasive
3. billboards
4. informative
6. advertisement
7. gadget
9. spot
10. sample
16. cable

Review 2, p. 107

1. advertisements
2. commercials
3. billboards
4. Slogans
5. brunch
6. spork
7. smog
8. motel
9. moped
10. Spanglish
11. informative
12. persuasive
13. offensive
14. negative
15. attractive